KB009467

후다닥 하룻밤에 끝내는

NEW SMART

상황별 영어
대표문장
3500

CHRIS SUH

MENT⊗RS

후다닥 하룻밤에 끝내는
상황별 영어 대표문장 3500

2024년 7월 22일 인쇄
2024년 12월 10일 2쇄 발행

지 은 이 Chris Suh
발 행 인 Chris Suh
발 행 처 **MENT❂RS**
경기도 성남시 분당구 분당로 53번길 12 313-1
TEL 031-604-0025 FAX 031-696-5221
mentors.co.kr
blog.naver.com/mentorsbook
* Play 스토어 및 App 스토어에서 '멘토스북' 검색해 어플다운받기!
등록일자 2005년 7월 27일
등록번호 제 2022-000130호
I S B N 979-11-980848-2-8
가 격 15,600원(MP3 무료다운로드)

잘못 인쇄된 책은 교환해 드립니다.
이 책에 게재된 내용의 일부 또는 전체를 무단으로 복제 및 발췌하는 것을 금합니다

PREFACE

Common Sentences
in Situation English

영어회화 상황별 대표문장 3500

가장 효율적인 영어회화 학습방법은 영어회화의 패턴을 집중적으로 익히는 것이고 그런 다음 그 패턴에 넣을 흔히 말하는 숙어라는 표현들을 왕창 습득해야 된다고 앞선 교재에서 필자는 누누이 강조하였다. 이 방법이 지름길이기는 하지만 계속 패턴과 숙어의 조합만으로 영어를 유창하게 말하는 것엔 한계가 있다. 영어표현들을 비슷한 상황에 맞게 구분 정리한 이번 책 〈후다닥 하룻밤에 끝내는 상황별 영어 대표문장 3500〉은 바로 그런 한계를 극복하고자 기획되었다.

외국인 회사에서 혹은 외국인 친구와의 대화를 할 때 혹은 비즈니스 상담을 할 때 등 그 어느 때보다 영어에 촘촘히 둘러싸여 있으며 그 어느 때보다 유창한 영어회화 실력이 필요한 때이다. 하지만 네이티브와 얘기를 나눠본 사람들은 다 동병상련이겠지만 하고 싶은 말을 어떻게 영어로 해야 할지 떠오르지 않아 그저 묵상만 할 때가 태반인 경우가 많을 것이다.

하고 싶은 말을 하지 못해 그저 묵상만 하고 있을 뿐일 때가 많아

그때그때 상황에 맞는 영어회화표현을 찾아낼 수 있어야

그건 우리 머릿 속에 충분한 영어회화표현 데이타베이스가 없기 때문이다. 기본데이터가 부족하다 보니 그때그때의 상황에 맞는 영어표현을 찾을 수가 없게 되는 것이다. 이 책 〈후다닥 하룻밤에 끝내는 상황별 영어 대표문장 3500〉은 포켓북으로 언제 어디서든 손에 들고 다니면서 바로 보고 바로 말할 수 있도록 3천 5백개 이상의 영어회화필수표현들을 일목요연하게 정리하였다. 교통, 관광, 전화, 식당, 문자, 메신저에서부터 약속, 충고, 부탁, 동의, 반대표현까지 언제 어디서나 네이티브에게 즉시 활용할 수 있는 현지 영어회화표현을 총집합하였다. 이렇게 상황에 맞게 지속적으로 그리고 반복적으로 그때그때 표현을 찾아보게 되다 보면 어느새 자신도 모르게 실용영어회화표현들이 머릿 속에 각인되어 영어 스피킹 실력이 늘어나게 될 것이다 .

다시한번 반복하지만 영어회화의 큰 기둥은 패턴+숙어의 조합으로 이를 놓쳐서는 안된다. 이를 중심으로 하여, 기본동사표현, 이디옴, 그리고 이 책처럼 상황별 등으로 영어회화에 다각적으로 접근해야 한다. 그래야만 영어회화학습의 지루함을 극복할 수도 있고 또한 중복학습을 통해서, 사서 매번 마무리하지 못하는 영어교재들의 한을 풀어 줄 수도 있을 것이다.

매번 마무리못하는 영어교재의 한을 풀어줘야

이 책의 특징

Common Sentences
in Situation English

❶ 영어회화에 빈출하는 표현들을 상황별로 총 3500개 이상 모아모아 정리하였다.

❷ 교통, 공항, 호텔, 식당, 전화, 비즈니스 등 물리적 상황에 따른 표현들을 구분하여 정리하였을 뿐만 아니라,

❸ 만남, 감사, 충고, 불만, 기쁨, 생각, 의견, 동의, 반대 등 추상적인 상황에 따른 표현들도 함께 모았다.

❹ 각 표현 아래에는 필요한 경우 보충설명이나 추가 예문을 넣어서 초보자의 이해를 더욱 쉽게 도모하였다.

❺ 모든 문장은 생동감 넘치는 원어민의 녹음이 되어 있어서 따라 읽으면서 실제 연습이 되도록 꾸며졌다.

이 책의 구성

Common Sentences
in Situation English

❶ 총 3500 여개의 문장들이 Chapter별 상황으로 구분 정리되어 있다.

❷ Chapter별 상황 구성은 다음과 같다.
물리적 상황은
Chapter 01 교통, 도로에서부터
Chapter 08 비즈니스 상황까지

그리고 추상적 상황은
Chapter 09 숫자, 연애에서부터
Chapter 17 동의, 반대까지
전체적으로 총 17개의 Chapter로 대분되어 나뉘어져 있다.

❸ 필요한 경우에는 상황에 자주 쓰이는 어구들을 Note라는 제목하에 정리하여 이해를 더욱 쉽게 하였다.

이책을 쉽게 보는 법

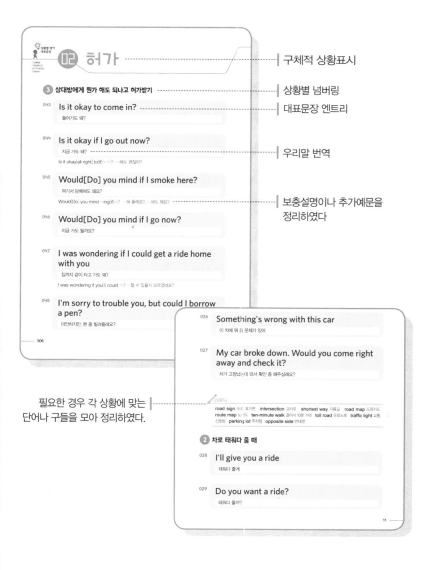

상황별 영어
대표문장

02 허가 ┄┄┄┄┄┄┄┄ 구체적 상황표시

Common
Sentences
in Situation
English

3 상대방에게 뭔가 해도 되냐고 허가받기 ┄┄┄┄┄┄┄ 상황별 넘버링

043 **Is it okay to come in?** ┄┄┄┄┄┄┄┄┄┄ 대표문장 엔트리

들어가도 돼?

044 **Is it okay if I go out now?**

지금 가도 돼? ┄┄┄┄┄┄┄┄┄┄┄┄┄┄ 우리말 번역

Is it okay[all right] to[if] ~ ~? ~해도 괜찮아?

045 **Would[Do] you mind if I smoke here?**

여기서 담배피도 돼요?

Would[Do] you mind ~ing[if] ~? ~해 줄래요?, ~해도 돼요? ┄┄┄┄ 보충설명이나 추가예문을
정리하였다

046 **Would[Do] you mind if I go now?**

지금 가도 될까요?

047 **I was wondering if I could get a ride home with you**

집까지 같이 타고 가도 돼?

I was wondering if you[I] could ~ ~할 수 있을지 모르겠네요?

048 **I'm sorry to trouble you, but could I borrow a pen?**

미안하지만, 펜 좀 빌려줄래요?

026 **Something's wrong with this car**

이 차에 뭐 좀 문제가 있어

027 **My car broke down. Would you come right away and check it?**

차가 고장났는데 와서 확인 좀 해주실래요?

필요한 경우 각 상황에 맞는
단어나 구들을 모아 정리하였다.

road sign 도시 표지판   intersection 교차로   shortest way 지름길   road map 도로지도
route map 노선도   ten-minute walk 걸어서 10분 거리   toll road 유료도로   traffic light 교통
신호등   parking lot 주차장   opposite side 반대편

2 차로 태워다 줄 때

028 **I'll give you a ride**

태워다 줄게

029 **Do you want a ride?**

태워다 줄까?

CONTENTS 🎎

Common Sentences
in Situation English

Common Sentences
in Situation English

Chapter

01

교통 · 도로

 교통

02 도로

교통

1 차가 너무 막힐 때

001 I'm stuck in traffic

길이 막혀 꼼짝못해

002 I got stuck in traffic on the way

도중에 차가 막혔어

003 Traffic is very heavy today

오늘 차가 너무 막혀

004 This is quite a traffic jam

교통이 꽉 막혔네

005 Traffic was bumper-to-bumper

차가 엄청 막혔어

006 It's a one-way street

일방 도로야

007 It's a right-turn-only lane

우회전 전용차선야

008 **This is a toll road**

유료도로야

009 **Why don't you slow down a bit?**

좀 천천히 가자

010 **I got caught speeding**

속도위반으로 걸렸어

011 **I was busted for speeding**

속도위반하다 걸렸어

012 **I just got my license**

방금 면허증 땄어

013 **Don't fall asleep at the wheel**

운전 중에 졸지 마라

014 **Be sure to drive carefully**

운전 조심하고

015 **Want me to take the wheel?**

내가 운전할까?

016

Fill it up

기름 가득 넣어줘요

017

Where can we fill it up?

어디서 기름넣지?

018

I ran out of gas

기름이 떨어졌어

019

Can you give me $10 worth of gas?

10달러어치 기름 넣어줄래요?

020

Would you change the oil, please?

엔진오일 갈아줄래요?

021

The engine won't start

차가 시동이 안 걸려요

022

Is it all right to park on the road?

도로에 주차해도 괜찮아?

023

Is there any gas station near here?

주변에 주유소 있어?

024 The brakes don't work
브레이크가 말을 안들어

025 I've got a flat
타이어가 빵구났어

026 Something's wrong with this car
이 차에 뭐 좀 문제가 있어

027 My car broke down. Would you come right away and check it?
차가 고장났는데 와서 확인 좀 해주실래요?

road sign 도로 표지판   intersection 교차로   shortest way 지름길   road map 도로지도
route map 노선도   ten-minute walk 걸어서 10분 거리   toll road 유료도로   traffic light 교통
신호등   parking lot 주차장   opposite side 반대편

2 차로 태워다 줄 때

028 I'll give you a ride
태워다 줄게

029 Do you want a ride?
태워다 줄까?

030 How about a ride?

태워줄래?

031 Are you going my way?

혹시 같은 방향으로 가니?, 같은 방향이면 태워줄래?

032 Hop in

어서 타

033 Where can I get a taxi?

택시 어디서 타나요?

034 Where's the taxi stand?

택시승강장이 어디예요?

035 Is there a taxi stand near here?

택시승강장이 이 근처에 있나요?

036 Can you get me a taxi, please?

택시 좀 잡아줄래요?

037 Can you call a cab for me?

택시 좀 불러줄래요?

038 **Where to?**

어디로 가세요?

039 **Where're you going?**

어디 가세요?

040 **(Take me) To this address, please**

이 주소로 가 주세요

041 **I'd like to go to this address**

이 주소로 갈려고요

042 **Please take me here**

이쪽으로 가 주세요

043 **Please take me to the airport**

공항으로 갑시다

044 **Here're twenty dollars, and keep the change**

여기 20달러예요, 거스름돈은 가져요

045 **Please stop just before that traffic light**

신호등 바로 전에 세워주세요

046

Pull over here

여기 세워줘요

047

Let me out of here

여기서 내릴게요

048

I get off here

여기서 내릴게요

049

Are we almost there?

거의 다 왔나요?

050

I have to get there by 8 o'clock. Could you hurry up?

8시까지 가야 되는데 서둘러 줄래요?

051

Clear the way!

비켜주세요!

052

Step aside

비켜주세요

053

Coming through

좀 지나갈게요

3 차를 렌트할 때

054
I'd like to rent a car, please
차를 렌트하려고요

055
I'd like to rent this car for 10 hours
10시간 동안 이 차를 렌트하려고요

056
Where can I rent a car?
차를 어디서 렌트할 수 있어요?

057
Where's the nearest rent-a-car company?
가까운 렌터카 회사가 어디죠?

058
What's the rental fee?
렌탈비가 얼마예요?

059
Here is my international driving license
여기 국제 운전면허증요

060
How much is the rate?
요금이 얼마예요?

061
Please show me the price list
가격표를 보여주세요

062

I only drive an automatic car

오토 차만 운전해요

063

With automatic transmission, please

오토차로 주세요

064

Do you deliver the car to my hotel?

호텔로 차를 갖다 주나요?

065

Where do I return the car?

차를 어디에 반납하나요?

066

Do I have to return the car filled with gas?

기름채워 반납해야 하나요?

067

Does this price include the insurance fee?

보험포함된 가격인가요?

068

Please give me insurance coverage

보험들어주세요

069

I'd like to buy insurance

보험가입할게요

070 **Full insurance, please**

보험 다 들어주세요

071 **Please tell me who I contact if I have troubles**

문제발생하면 누구와 연락해야 하죠?

072 **Where should I call, if I have any trouble?**

문제생기면 어디에 연락해야죠?

073 **How long will you need it?**

얼마동안 쓰실 건가요?

074 **Which model do you like?**

어떤 모델을 좋아하세요?

075 **An automatic, medium-sized car**

중형의 오토차로 해주세요

076 **Can I leave the car at my destination?**

목적지에 차를 두어도 됩니까?

COMMON
SENTENCES
IN SITUATION
ENGLISH

NOTE

be looking for …을 찾고 있다 walk down …을 따라 걸어가다 be[get] lost 길을 잃다 go back 되돌아가다 get (to) + 장소 …에 가다, 도착하다(arrive at) get off (기차 등 대중 교통 수단에서) 내리다 take the subway 지하철을 타다 be close to + 장소 …에 가깝다 go straight 곧장 가다 switch buses 버스를 갈아타다 make a turn 방향을 틀다 turn around (반대쪽으로) 방향을 바꾸다 turn the corner 모퉁이를 돌다 follow …를 따라 가다 head …로 향해 가다 be located 위치하다 show A the way A에게 길을 안내하다 write the directions down 가는 방법을 적다

④ 버스나 전철을 타거나 내릴 때

077 Where's the bus stop?

버스 정거장이 어디예요?

078 Which way is the bus stop?

버스 정거장이 어느 편에 있나요?

079 May I have a subway route map?

지하철 노선도 좀 주실래요?

080 Do you have a train schedule?

열차시간표 있어요?

081 Is there a direct train to New York?

뉴욕행 직행열차 있어요?

082 Where is the ticket counter?

매표소가 어디인가요?

083 # A single ticket to New York, please

뉴욕행 편도 주세요

084 # How much is the (bus) fare?

요금이 얼마예요?

085 # How much to downtown?

시내까지 얼마인가요?

086 # Which train should I take to Kangnam?

강남가려면 어떤 전철을 타야 돼요?

087 # Which train goes to Kangnam?

어느 전철이 강남가요?

088 # Which bus goes to the center of town?

어떤 버스가 시내중심으로 가나요?

089 # What time is the last train to Suwon?

수원행 막차는 몇시에 있어요?

090 # Which bus goes to Chicago?

어떤 버스가 시카고로 가나요?

091 Is this a right train for Boston?

이게 보스톤 가는 기차 맞나요?

092 Does this train stop at Incheon?

이 전철이 인천에서 서나요?

093 Does this bus go to Sears Tower?

이 버스가 시어스 타워에 가나요?

094 How many stops are there to Kyungbokgung?

경복궁까지 몇 정거장예요?

095 How many stops to the museum?

박물관까지 몇 정거장입니까?

096 Where am I supposed to change[transfer]?

어디서 갈아타야 하나요?

097 You can change to Line #3 at Yaksu

약수역에서 3호선으로 갈아타세요

098 Take this train

이 열차를 타세요

099   Take the orange train

오렌지 색 열차를 타세요

100   How often do trains come?

열차 배차시간이 어떻게 돼요?

101   The trains come every ten minutes

열차들은 10분마다 와요

102   Could you tell me when to get off?

어디서 내려야하는지 알려줄래요?

103   It's four stops from here

여기서부터 4정거장에서요

104   After the next stop

다음 정거장 후에요

105   What's the next stop[station]?

다음 정거장은 어디예요?

106   The next stop is Sadang

다음 정거장은 사당이예요

107 Do I have to transfer?

갈아타야 합니까?

108 You have to change trains at the next station

다음 정거장에서 갈아타야 돼요

109 What time does the bus for New York leave?

뉴욕행 버스가 언제 출발해요?

110 I went past my stop

내릴 곳을 지나쳤어요

111 How can I go back to East Hill station?

이스트 힐 역으로 어떻게 다시 돌아가요?

112 I'd like a hotel near the station

역에서 가까운 호텔로 가주세요

113 What time does the next bus leave?

다음 버스가 언제 출발합니까?

114 What time does the last train leave?

막차가 언제 출발합니까?

115 Is there any seat in the non-smoking car?

비흡연석에 좌석 좀 있어요?

5 길을 잃었을 때 길 물어보기

116 Where am I?

여기가 어디죠?

117 Where am I on this map?

지도상에 제가 어디 있는 거죠?

118 I can't understand where I am on this map

지도상에 어딘지 모르겠어요

119 Well, this is Baker St., which is right here on the map

글쎄요, 이곳이 베이커 가(街)니까, 지도에서는 바로 여기네요

120 What's the name of this street?

여기 거리명이 어떻게 됩니까?

121 I think I'm lost

길을 잃은 것 같아요

122
Excuse me, but I'm lost

실례합니다만, 길을 잃어서요

123
I'm trying to go to COEX, but I think I'm lost

코엑스가려는데 길을 잃은 것 같아요

124
I got lost

길을 잃었어요

125
I seem to have lost my way

제가 길을 잃은 것 같아요

126
Is this the right road to reach Wall Street?

이 길이 월스트리트로 가는 길 맞나요?

127
Is this the right way to go to Mapo?

이 길이 마포가는 길 맞아요?

128
Does this road go to the station?

이 길이 역으로 향하나요?

129
Am I on the right road for the Korean Stock Exchange?

증권거래소 가는 길 맞나요?

130 Which way is it to the Blue House?

어느 길이 청와대로 가나요?

131 Could you draw me a map?

약도 좀 그려줄래요?

상황별 영어 대표문장

COMMON
SENTENCES
IN SITUATION
ENGLISH

02 도로

6 길을 몰라 알려주지 못할 때

132 **I'm a stranger here myself**

여기가 초행길이라서요, 여기는 처음 와봐서요

133 **I'm sorry, but I'm a stranger here too**

미안하지만 저도 여긴 잘 몰라요

134 **Sorry, I'm new here too**

미안하지만 저도 여기가 초행길이어서요

135 **I'm not familiar with this area**

이 지역은 잘 몰라요

136 **Where do you want to go?**

어디에 가실 건데요?

137 **Where is it that you are heading?**

어디 가는 길인데요?

138 **Are you lost?**

길을 잃었나요?

139 I think you're heading in the wrong direction

방향을 잘못 잡은 것 같은데요

140 If you get lost, just give me a call

혹 길을 잃어버리면 전화주세요

141 Why don't you ask someone else?

다른 사람한테 물어보세요

142 I'm sorry, but I'm not from Seoul

미안하지만 서울 사람이 아니라서요

143 I'm not a local

이 지역 사람이 아니에요

144 I'm not from around here

나도 여기 잘 몰라요

145 This is my first time here too

여기 나도 처음야

146 Wait a minute, let me ask someone for you

잠깐, 딴사람한테 물어볼게요

영어가 안될 때는 "I'm sorry, but I can't speak English very well" 혹은 "I'm sorry, but my English isn't very good"이라 한 후 "Could you ask someone else?"나 "You'd better check with someone else"라고 하면 된다

27

NOTE

in the wrong direction 잘못된 방향으로, 틀린 방향으로 timetable 시각표 direct bus 직행버스 fare 요금 express charge 급행요금 conductor 승무원 dining car 식당차 sleeping car 침대차 upper[lower] berth 상층[하층]침대

7 구체적으로 길을 알려달라고 할 때

147 **Can you tell me how to get to the nearest subway station?**

가장 가까운 지하철역 좀 알려줄래요?

148 **Can you tell me the way to Maxim?**

맥심사 가는 길 좀 가르쳐 줄래요?

149 **Do you know the shortest way to the mall?**

쇼핑몰가는 지름길 아세요?

150 **Do you know any good outlet malls in Buffalo?**

버팔로에 좋은 아울렛몰 좀 알아?

151 **Where is the nearest post office?**

가장 가까운 우체국이 어디예요?

152 **I'm looking for the convention center**

컨벤션 센터를 찾고 있는데요

153

I'm trying to find the National Art Gallery

국립 미술관에 가려구요

154

How long does it take to get to the stadium?

경기장까지 시간이 얼마나 걸리죠?

155

How do[can] I get there?

거기에 어떻게 가죠?

156

Is it within walking distance?

걸어서 가도 되나요?

157

Can I get there by bus?

버스로 갈 수 있나요?

158

How far is it to Busan?

부산까지 얼마나 걸려요?

159

How far is it from the subway to the museum?

전철역에서 박물관까지 얼마나 걸려요?

160

I was wondering if you could tell me where to get off the train

어느 역에서 내려야 하는지 알려줄래요?

161 How far is it from here?

여기서 얼마나 먼가요?

162 Is it far (from here)?

(여기서) 멀어요?

163 Is Busan far?

부산이 멀리 있나요?

164 Is it close[near] to Kyungbu Highway?

경부고속도로까지 가까워?

165 Am I near[close to] Busan?

부산에 가까이 왔나요?

166 What's the fastest way to get there?

거기까지 가는데 뭐가 가장 빠른 길이야?

167 What's the best way to get there?

거기 가는데 가장 좋은 방법은 뭐야?

168 Which way is shorter?

어느 길이 더 빨라?

169 Is it on the right or left?

오른편에 있나요, 왼편에 있나요?

NOTE

How far is it from A to B? A에서 B까지 얼마나 멉니까?   How long does it take to + V?
…하는 데 시간이 얼마나 걸리죠?   How do I get to + 장소? …에 어떻게 가나요?   Do you know
how to get to + 장소? …에 어떻게 가는지 아세요?   how to get to + 장소 …에 가는 방법   the
fastest way to + 장소 …에 가는 가장 빠른 방법

8 구체적으로 길 알려주기(1)

170 Go down this street and turn to the left

이 길로 내려가서 왼쪽으로 도세요

171 Go straight for two blocks

두 블록 더 곧장 가요

172 Go straight on the highway for ten kilometers

고속도로를 타고 10킬로 곧장 가요

173 Go east for two blocks and then turn right

동쪽으로 2블록 간후 우회전해요

174 Keep going straight until you reach the church

교회까지 곧장 가요

176 Take this road for about five minutes and it's on your left

이 길로 5분가면 왼편에 있어요

177 Take[Follow] this road

이 길을 따라가요

176 Take this road until it ends and then turn right

이 길 끝에서 우회전해요

178 Take Line #3 and get off at Shinsa Station

3호선 타고 신사역에서 내려요

179 Take the subway for one stop and get off at Yoksam Station

지하철로 한 정거장 가서 역삼역에서 내려요

180 Take the subway from Bloor Station and get off at King Station

블로어 역에서 지하철을 타고 킹 역에서 내리면 돼요

181 Take bus number 65 and get off at the third stop

65번 타고 3번째 정거장에서 내려요

182 Turn right at the first traffic light

첫번째 신호등에서 우회전해요

183 Turn left[right] at the first intersection

첫번째 교차로에서 좌(우)회전해요

184 Turn to the left when you come to a post office

우체국에서 좌회전해요

185 Go back that way for ten minutes and take the road on your left

왔던 길을 10분정도 되돌아간 다음 왼쪽 도로를 타세요

9 구체적으로 길 알려주기(2)

186 It's a ten minute walk from here

여기서 걸어서 10분 거리에 있어요

걸어서 5분 거리는 five-minute walk로 five와 minute 사이에 '-' 를 붙여야 하지만 현대의 바쁜 영어에서는 생략하여 five minute walk로 쓰기도 한다.

187 It's about 10 minutes on foot

걸어서 10분 정도 걸려요

188 Even on foot, it's no more than 10 minutes

걸어도 10분 이상 안 걸려요

189 It should take 20 minutes by car

차로 20분 정도 걸릴거예요

190 The museum is ten kilometers west of City Hall

박물관은 시청 서쪽 10킬로 지점에 있어

'A' is + 거리 + west[east] of~ 'A'가 …의 서(동)쪽 거리만큼에 있어

191 The hospital is a five minute walk from the bus stop

병원은 정거장에서 걸어서 5분걸려

'A' is + 시간 + walk[ride] from~ 'A'가 …에서 걸어서[차타고] ~분[시간]거리야

192 It's not far from here

여기서 멀지 않아요

193 It's not (that) far

(그렇게) 멀지 않아요

194 It's on the right

오른편에 있어요

195 It's around the corner, to your left

왼편 모퉁이를 돌면 있습니다

196 It's just down the hall to your left

복도를 내려가다 보면 왼편에 있어요

197 You'll see it on your right side

오른편에 있을거예요

198 You can't miss it

쉽게 찾을 수 있을거예요

199 I'm going in that direction

저도 그 쪽으로 가는 중이에요

200 I'm going there myself

저도 그리로 가는 중이에요

201 I'll show you the way myself

제가 직접 안내할게요

202 Let me show you the way

제가 길을 알려드릴게요

203 Do you want me to take you there?

제가 거기까지 모셔다 드릴까요?

Chapter

02

공항 · 비행

상황별 영어 대표문장

01 탑승

NOTE

book a flight 비행편을 예약하다   change[cancel] one's flight 비행편 예약을 변경[취소]하다   one-way ticket 편도 항공권(cf. round-trip ticket 왕복항공권)   open ticket 비행편 시간을 필요에 따라 변경할 수 있는 항공권   reconfirm 예약을 확인하다   reserve a seat for a flight to …행 비행기 좌석을 예약하다   return date 돌아오는 날짜(cf. date of departure 출발일)   no-show 비행편을 예약하고 탑승하지 않는 사람   boarding pass 탑승권   international flights 국제선   domestic flights 국내선   transit passenger 비행기 환승객(cf. transit lounge 환승 대기실)

1 비행기 표 예약하기

001

I'd like to make a reservation for June 13th

6월 13일로 예약하고 싶은데요

002

Smoking or non-smoking?

흡연석으로 하시겠어요, 비흡연석으로 하시겠어요?

003

I would prefer non-smoking

비흡연석으로 주세요

004

Okay, and I have an aisle seat for you

알겠습니다, 통로측으로 드리죠

005

Are there any seats left on the 10 o'clock flight to LA?

10시 LA행 좌석 남았나요?

006

Could you tell me if you have any seats available to Miami?

마이애미행 비행편에 남아있는 좌석이 있습니까?

007

I have a couple of seats left on this afternoon flight

오늘 오후 비행편에 두 자리가 남아 있습니다

008

I'm on the waiting list

난 대기자 명단에 있어요

009

Round trip or one-way?

왕복권요 아니면 편도요?

010

I'd like a round-trip ticket to New York

뉴욕행 왕복 항공권 주세요

011

When would you like to depart and return?

언제 출발해서 언제 돌아오실 생각이십니까?

012

I'd like to leave this Monday and return on Sunday

이번 월요일에 출발해서 일요일에 돌아오려구요

013

All of the flights are full

모든 항공편이 예약만료되었어요

014

All of the other flights were booked solid

다른 항공편이 다 예약되었어요

015

Do you know when the next flight leaves?

다음 비행기는 언제죠?

016

How much is business class?

비즈니스 클래스 요금이 얼마죠?

017

Do you want first class, business or coach class?

일등석, 비즈니스 아니면 보통석으로 드릴까요?

018

I'm booked on AA Flight 567 to NY

뉴욕행 AA567편을 예약했는데요

019

I'd like to change my flight

비행편을 바꾸고 싶습니다

020

May I change my return date to May 7th?

돌아오는 날짜를 5/7일로 변경해줄래요?

021

Could I please have your name, flight number and date of departure?

성함과 비행편 번호를 말씀해 주시겠습니까? 그리고 출발일도요

021

Unfortunately, there are no seats available at this moment, but I could put you on a waiting list

안됐지만 지금 현재로서는 남아있는 좌석이 없습니다. 대기자 명단에라도 올려드릴까요?

023

What is your flight number?

비행편 번호가 어떻게 되시죠?

024

It is 845, to New York

845번, 뉴욕행입니다

025

Your reservation is confirmed, but the flight may be delayed because of bad weather

예약이 확인되었습니다. 그런데 날씨가 나빠서 늦게 출발할지도 모르겠어요

026

I'd like to reconfirm my flight

예약을 다시 확인하려구요

027

I want to reconfirm my reservation

예약을 확인하려구요

028 I'd like to change my reservation, please

예약을 변경하려구요

029 I'd like to cancel my reservation for the flight on March 5th to Seoul, flight number KW 009, and change it to March 7th, flight number KW 008 instead, please

서울행 3월 5일 비행편 KW009 예약을 취소하고 대신 3월 7일 KW008편으로 바꿔주세요

030 Can I change my reservation to a later [earlier] flight?

예약을 좀 늦은[빠른] 비행편으로 바꿀 수 있나요?

2 짐 부치기

031 How can I get to the check-in counter (for Japan Air Lines)?

(일본항공) 탑승수속 카운터로 어떻게 가죠?

032 You need to go up one level and it is on the north side of the building

한 층 올라가면 건물 북쪽 편에 있습니다

033 Is the flight leaving on time?

비행기가 제 시간에 출발하나요?

034 # Do you have any luggage to check?

부치실 짐이 있으십니까?

035 # How many pieces of luggage are you checking in?

부칠 짐이 몇 개죠?

036 # How many bags do you want to check?

가방을 몇개 부칠 건가요?

037 # I would like to check three pieces

세개를 부치려고 하는데요

038 # Is that your carry-on?

저게 갖고 타실 짐인가요?

039 # How many pieces of carry-on are you going to take?

몇개를 갖고 타실 건가요?

040 # You're only allowed two, but you may be able to take one as a carry-on

두개까지만 부치실 수 있습니다. 하지만 하나는 휴대 수하물로 들고 타도 됩니다

041 # Your luggage is over the maximum weight

짐이 수하물 제한한도를 초과했습니다

042 # Fortunately, your bags are within the maximum allowable weight

손님의 짐이 무게 한도를 넘지 않아서 다행입니다

043 # How much over is it?

얼마나 넘었죠?

044 # It's five kilograms over the weight allowance

5킬로 초과하셨네요

045 # I'll put a fragile sticker on it for you

짐에 취급주의 스티커를 붙여 드리죠

046 # I'm just taking my carry-on

비행기에 들고 탈 짐밖에 없습니다

NOTE

check-in 탑승수속(cf. check in 탑승수속을 하다) **carry-on (baggage)** 기내 휴대 수하물
excess baggage charge 화물 중량초과 요금 **free (baggage) allowance** 무료로 부칠 수
있는 짐의 한도 **personal belongings[effects]** 개인 소지품 **luggage cart** 화물 운반용 수레
prohibited item[articles] 소지 금지목록 **baggage claim area** 수하물 찾는 곳 **baggage
check** 탑승 전 짐을 부칠 때 받은 수하물표 **carousel** 수하물 운반대. 공항에서 승객들이 짐을 찾아갈
수 있도록 회전하는 수하물 운반대를 말한다 **lost luggage counter** 화물 분실 신고대 **security
check** 보안검색 **walk-through detector** 소지 금지목록을 검사하기 위해 걸어서 통과하는 검색장
치(cf. hand-held detector 손에 들고 쓰는 검색장치)

3 탑승수속 및 탑승구 찾기

047
Please place all metal objects in the tray
금속물건은 전부 받침대에 꺼내 놓으세요

048
Do I need to take off my belt because of its metal buckle?
금속으로 된 버클이 달린 혁대도 풀어놓아야 하나요?

049
You can collect your belongings on the other side of the machine
운반대 저쪽 끝에서 손님의 개인 소지품을 찾아가시면 됩니다

050
Do you have any prohibited items with you?
금지품목을 소지하고 계세요?

051
Did anyone ask you to bring anything into the country for them?
누군가가 손님에게 뭔가 가져다 달라고 부탁한 게 있습니까?

052

No, these are all my own personal belongings

아뇨, 이것들은 전부 다 제 개인 물품들입니다

053

You can't bring your pet with you

애완동물은 데리고 탈 수 없어요

054

Would you mind letting me check your bag?

손님 가방 속을 확인해 봐도 될까요?

055

What's this red stuff?

이 빨간 건 뭐죠?

056

That's hot pepper paste, a kind of Korean traditional sauce. Is it one of the prohibited items?

고추장입니다. 한국 전통 소스의 일종이죠. 그게 금지 품목입니까?

057

I'm afraid that this is not permitted

이건 가져가실 수 없겠는데요

058

Your plane is now boarding

손님 비행기가 지금 탑승 중입니다

059

Your plane is now boarding at gate 3

손님 비행기는 지금 3번 게이트에서 탑승 중입니다

060

You must proceed to boarding gate 3 immediately

지금 곧바로 3번 탑승구로 가셔야 합니다

061

Could you tell me how to get to Gate 3?

3번 게이트로 어떻게 가죠?

062

Where's the boarding gate?

탑승구가 어딥니까?

063

Excuse me. How do I get to Gate 43?

죄송하지만 43번 게이트를 어떻게 가죠?

064

Which gate is for the flight to Washington?

워싱톤 행 비행편은 어느 게이트로 가야 하나요?

065

I think if you follow those signs you'll get there

저 표시들을 따라가시면 그리 가실 수 있을거예요

066

What time do you start boarding?

탑승은 언제 하나요?

067

Has this flight begun boarding?

이 항공편 탑승 시작했나요?

상황별 영어
대표문장

COMMON
SENTENCES
IN SITUATION
ENGLISH

 **02 기내**

NOTE

in-flight service 기내 서비스(cf. in-flight movie 기내 상영영화)   flight attendant (기내) 승무원
air duty-free shopping guide 기내 면세품 안내책자   airsickness bag 비행기 멀미용 봉투
refreshments 비행 중에 제공되는 간단한 음식과 음료

---

4 기내에서 이런저런

068 **Could I get a copy of the Wall Street Journal?**

월스트리트 한 부좀 줄래요?

069 **Unfortunately, we don't have any left**

죄송합니다만, 남은 게 없습니다

070 **What other papers do you have?**

다른 신문은 어떤 게 있죠?

071 **What are my choices for breakfast?**

아침 메뉴가 어떤 게 있죠?

072 **We have a vegetarian omelet or ham and eggs**

야채 오믈릿과 햄에 계란을 곁들인 요리가 있습니다

073 **I'd like the ham and eggs please**

햄과 계란 요리가 좋겠군요

074
Do you want some coffee or something with that?

커피 같은 것도 함께 드릴까요?

075
What would you like for dinner, beef or fish?

저녁으로 고기와 생선 중 어느 걸로 하실래요?

076
What would you like to drink?

뭘 드실래요?

077
I'd like a glass of milk

우유 한 잔 주십시오

078
Coffee, please

커피 주세요

079
With sugar and cream?

설탕과 프림 넣고요?

080
Can I have some water?

물 좀 줄래요?

081
Can I have some medicine?

약 좀 줄래요?

082

Could you tell me how to fill out this form?

이 서식 쓰는 거 알려줄래요?

083

Can you help me with this form?

이 서식 쓰는 것 좀 도와줄래요?

084

Will you show me how to turn on the light?

불 어떻게 키는지 알려줄래요?

085

Would you like me to close the shutter?

창문가리개를 내려 드릴까요?

086

Could I please get a blanket?

담요 한 장 갖다주시겠어요?

087

This isn't your seat, I'm afraid

잘못 앉으신 것 같은데요

088

The earphones aren't working

이어폰이 작동 안돼요

089

This is my first time flying and I want to know where the washroom is

이번에 비행기를 처음 타보는데요, 화장실이 어딘지 모르겠네요

090

Can I use the washroom now?

지금 화장실을 사용해도 되나요?

091

You'll have to wait until the plane takes off and the captain shuts off the fasten-seat-belt sign

비행기가 이륙해서 기장님이 안전벨트를 묶고 있으라는 신호를 끄고 난 후에 이용하시면 됩니다

092

I can't believe how cheap the prices are. I'm going to get a bottle of whisky and some perfume

가격이 정말 싸군요. 위스키 한 병하고 향수를 좀 살게요

093

How would you like to pay for that? You may use your credit card

지불은 어떻게 하시겠습니까? 신용카드를 사용하셔도 됩니다

094

I'd like to pay in cash. How much is it?

현금으로 할게요. 얼마죠?

상황별 영어
대표문장

COMMON
SENTENCES
IN SITUATION
ENGLISH

03 환승

NOTE

be delayed (비행편의 출발이) 지연되다   departure time 비행기 출발시간   morning
[afternoon] flight 아침[오후] 비행편   domestic[international] line 국내[국제]선   take off
(비행기가) 이륙하다(↔touch down, land)   ahead of schedule 예정보다 빨리(↔behind schedule)
boarding time 탑승시간   departure time 출발시간   delayed arrival 연착

5 비행기를 갈아타지 못했을 때

095

I need to catch my connecting flight

연결 비행편을 타려고 하는데요

096

I missed my connecting flight to NY

뉴욕행 연결 비행편을 놓쳤어요

097

I missed AA 456 to New York because of the delay of plane from Incheon

인천출발 비행편 연착으로 뉴욕행 AA456를 놓쳤어요

098

I need to catch my connecting flight. Could you tell me where gate K is?

비행기를 갈아타려는데요. K탑승구가 어디 있는지 알려줄래요?

099

That gate is not in this terminal, it's in Terminal Two

K탑승구는 이 터미널에 없구요, 제 2터미널에 있어요

100

Do you happen to know when the next available flight leaves?

혹시 다음 비행기는 언제 있는지 아세요?

101

Let me check. It looks like we can put you on a flight in about an hour

확인해보죠. 한 시간 후쯤 출발하는 비행기에 자리를 마련할 수 있을 것 같네요

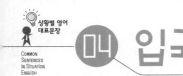

상황별 영어
대표문장

COMMON
SENTENCES
IN SITUATION
ENGLISH

04 입국

6 도착해서 입국할 때 쓰는 표현들

102
May I see your passport, please?

여권 좀 보여주시겠습니까?

103
Good morning, may I have your ticket and your passport, please?

안녕하세요, 비행기표와 여권을 주시겠습니까?

104
We are on a group tour. So the tour conductor has all our tickets

단체여행중입니다. 여행가이드가 우리 티켓을 모두 갖고 있어요

105
Would you show me the return ticket?

돌아갈 항공권 보여주시겠어요?

106
Do you have a return ticket?

돌아갈 항공권 있어요?

107
How long are you planning to stay in the US?

미국엔 얼마나 머물 계획예요?

108
Where will you be staying?

어디 머무를 예정입니까?

109 I plan to stay for a week

일주일간 머물겁니다

110 I'm going to stay for a couple of months

몇달간 머물려구요

111 I'm planning to stay for three weeks and then I'm leaving the country

3주간 있다가 떠날 생각이에요

112 What's the purpose of your visit?

방문 목적이 뭡니까?

113 What brought you here?

여기 오신 이유는요?

114 What's the nature of your visit to the US?

미국엔 무슨 일로 오셨나요?

115 I'm here to see some of my relatives

친척들을 좀 만나려고 왔어요

116 I'm visiting on business

업무차 왔어요

117 I'm going to New York on business

업무차 뉴욕에 왔습니다

118 Business

업무차요

119 I'm here on business

사업차 왔어요

120 I'm here on vacation

휴가차 왔어요

121 I came here to study

공부하러 왔습니다

122 I will stay with my friend in New York

뉴욕의 친구와 함께 머물겁니다

123 I'm going to stay in New York, but I haven't decided the hotel yet

뉴욕에 머물거지만 아직 호텔을 정하진 않았습니다

124 I'll attend a language school

어학원을 다닐겁니다

125 **I'll visit a friend in Chicago**

시카고에 있는 친구를 만나러 왔어요

126 **Sightseeing**

관광요

127 **Can you tell me where you're going to stay?**

여행 기간 동안 어디에 계실 건가요?

128 **Can you tell me where you're going to be staying for the duration of your trip?**

여행 기간 동안 어디에 계실 건가요?

129 **Where are you staying?**

어디 머무실거예요?

130 **I'm staying at the Intercontinental Hotel**

인터콘티넨탈 호텔에 머물거예요

131 **My company has booked me a room at the Park Plaza Hotel and I'll be staying there for the next week**

회사에서 파크플라자 호텔에 방을 예약해둬서 다음 주에는 거기에 있을거예요

132 I'm staying at a home in Washington. Here's the address of my host family

워싱톤의 집에서 머물겁니다. 이게 내가 머물 집의 주소입니다

NOTE

immigration 입국 심사 **immigration office** 입국관리사무소 **declare** (세관에) 신고하다(cf. **custom declaration** 세관 신고서) **clear customs** 세관을 통과하다 **fill out a form** 양식서를 작성하다 **disembarkation[entry] card** 입국 신고서 **customs declaration form** 세관신고서 **nationality** 국적 **family name** 성 **first name** 이름

7 신고할 물건 확인할 때

133 (Do you have) Anything to declare?

신고할 물건이 있습니까?

134 I am bringing some traditional Korean food with me

한국 전통 음식을 좀 가지고 들어왔는데요

135 I bought it at the duty-free counter in the airport in Seoul. It's a gift for my friend

서울에 있는 공항 면세점에서 샀어요. 친구에게 줄 선물입니다

136 I have two gifts for friends

친구에게 줄 선물이 2개 있습니다

137 What is the approximate value?

대략 값어치가 어떻게 됩니까?

138 What is their value?

가격이 어떻게 돼요?

139 How much money do you have?

돈은 얼마나 소지하고 있습니까?

140 I have about $2,000 dollars

한 2천 달러 갖고 있습니다

141 I have this camera that I bought for my friend

내가 친구줄려고 산 카메라입니다

142 How much did you pay for it?

얼마주고 사셨습니까?

143 I can't find my baggage

내 가방을 못 찾겠어요

144 You need to go to the lost luggage counter

수화물 분실신고대로 가보세요

145 Are you sure that you checked thoroughly around the carousel?

수하물 회전 운반대 주변을 샅샅이 찾아보셨어요?

146 I waited for an hour and there were no bags on or around the carousel

한 시간이나 기다렸지만 운반대 위는 물론이고 그 주변에도 없었다구요

147 If that's the case, you need to go to the lost luggage counter which is located at the end of this hall

그렇다면 이 복도 끝에 있는 수하물 분실 신고대로 가보세요

148 I'm still suffering from jet lag

아직 시차가 적응이 안되었어요

149 I left something on the plane

비행기에 뭘 두고 왔어요

8 호텔에서 공항으로 갈 때

150 Excuse me. Could you tell me how to get to the Bedford hotel?

실례합니다. 베드포드 호텔에 어떻게 가는지 알려주시겠어요?

151 **You have a couple of choices, you can take an airport limo or a taxi**

두 가지 방법 중에 고르시면 돼요. 공항 리무진 버스나 택시 타는거죠

152 **What time does the limo leave?**

리무진 버스는 몇 시에 출발하나요?

153 **In about ten minutes. When your limo comes to get you, the driver will help you with your luggage**

한 10분쯤 후에요. 리무진을 탈 때 운전사가 짐을 실어줄거예요

154 **Do you have any tags?**

짐에 붙일 만한 꼬리표 있나요?

155 **I was wondering if you could tell me where the taxi stand is?**

택시 승차장이 어디에 있는지 알려주실래요?

156 **I think that it's at the other end of the terminal. Just follow the signs and you'll find it**

터미널 맞은 편에 있는 것 같아요. 저 표지판들만 따라가다 보면 나올거예요

157

I need to get to the Delta Inn

델타 인으로 가려고 하는데요

158

How long will it take for us to reach the Inn?

그 호텔 에 가는 데 얼마 걸리죠?

159

Do you need to put anything in the trunk?

짐을 트렁트에 넣으실래요?

160

Well, here we are. Let me unload your luggage for you

자, 다 왔습니다. 짐을 내려 드리죠

161

How much is the fare?

요금이 얼마죠?

162

Here's twenty dollars, and keep the change

여기 20달러예요. 거스름돈은 가지세요

163

Can you tell me how to get to the Ford Hotel?

포드호텔에 어떻게 가는지 알려줄래요?

164 **Where can I get a taxi to the Inter Continental Hotel?**

인터콘티넨탈에 가려면 어디서 택시를 타야 돼요?

165 **Would you take us to the Inter Continental Hotel?**

인터콘티넨탈로 데려다 줄래요?

Chapter

03

호텔 · 관광

이 호텔

NOTE

information desk 안내 데스크   (airport) limo 공항 리무진 버스(=limousine)   shuttle bus 일
정한 장소를 왕복 운행하는 셔틀버스   tag[label] 꼬리표(를 붙이다)   taxi stand 택시 승차장

1 예약없이 호텔 들어가기

001

I'd like a twin room for three night, please

3일 묵을 트윈룸을 부탁해요

002

Is there a room available for tonight?

오늘밤 방 있나요?

003

Do you have a room for tonight?

오늘밤 방 있어요?

004

What kind of room do you want?

어떤 종류의 방을 드릴까요?

005

Can you recommend any other hotel?

다른 호텔 추천해주실래요?

006

Would you refer me to another hotel?

다른 호텔 추천해줄래요?

007

How many nights?

몇일밤 묵을 실건가요?

008

Let me just check to see if a room is available for you

이용할 수 있는 방이 있는지 금방 확인해보도록 하죠

009

Just one night. How much does it cost?

하룻밤요. 얼마입니까?

010

What is the rate for a single room per night?

싱글룸으로 하룻밤 얼마입니까?

011

I want to stay for two nights

2박 3일 묵을 겁니다

012

Is there a cheaper room?

더 싼 방이 있나요?

013

Can I change my room?

방을 바꿀 수 있어요?

014

We have a single for 40 dollars per night

싱글룸은 하룻밤에 40달러입니다

015
I'd like the most inexpensive room you have for three nights

3박 4일 묵을 건데 가장 저렴한 방을 주세요

016
I'd like a room with an ocean view

바닷가가 보이는 방을 주세요

017
This room is too small. I'd like to change to a larger room, please

이 방은 너무 작네요. 큰 방으로 바꿔주세요

018
I'd like to change to a double room, please

더블룸으로 바꿔주세요

019
Where is the fire exit?

비상구가 어디인가요?

2 예약된 호텔에서 체크인하기

020
Does this rate include breakfast?

이 요금에 조식이 포함되어 있나요?

021
Check in, please

체크인 해주세요

022

I'd like to check in

체크인 할게요

023

When's the checking time?

체크인 타임이 언제인가요?

024

What time can I check in?

언제 체크인 하나요?

025

Your room won't be ready until 1 o'clock

한 시에 입실가능합니다

026

Can you keep my bags until I check in?

체크인 할 때까지 가방 좀 맡아주세요

027

The travel agency made a reservation for me

여행사가 예약을 해놨어요

028

I have a reservation

예약을 했는데요

029

I've reserved a single[double]

싱글(더블)룸 예약했습니다

030

I have a confirmed reservation

예약 확인했는데요

031

I reserved a room for tonight

오늘밤 예약했는데요

032

I have a reservation. I'm Sung-su Kim

예약했는데 김성수라고 합니다

033

Hi, my name is Ki-su Park and I'm here to check in

안녕하세요, 저는 박기수라고 하는데요. 체크인을 하려구요

034

I have your reservation. Are you still planning to stay the third night?

예약되어 있네요. 3일간 묵기로 되어 있는데, 변함없으신가요?

035

Yes, we have your name. Welcome to our hotel

네, 예약되어 있네요. 저희 호텔에 오셔서 반갑습니다

036

Sorry, but I can't find your name

죄송하지만, 성함이 없는데요

037

Your room number is 505. Here is the key

505호실 입니다. 여기 열쇠있습니다

038

Take my baggage, please

가방 좀 들어줘요

039

Can you keep my valuables?

귀중품을 맡길 수 있어요?

040

I'd like the key to room 1024, please

1024호 열쇠 좀 주세요

041

I'd like to leave my room key, please

키를 맡겨놓을려구요

042

Where is the dining room?

식당이 어디예요?

043

Where can I get some beer?

맥주는 어디서 살 수 있어요?

044

Could you recommend a place that will deliver to the hotel?

호텔로 시켜먹을 만한 곳을 추천해주실래요?

045 What time do you serve breakfast?

아침은 몇시에 먹을 수 있습니까?

046 What time does the dining room open?

식당은 언제 문 열어요?

047 You can call down to the reception at any time by dialing 0 on your phone

방 전화기의 0번을 누르시면 언제든 접수창구와 통화하실 수 있습니다

NOTE

check-in counter 호텔에 도착하여 체크인 절차를 밟는 곳 reservation[confirmation] slip 예약확인표 suite 호텔에서 침실 외에 거실 · 응접실 등이 딸려 있는 방 room won't be ready until + 시간 …시 이후에 방에 들어갈 수 있다 room service 룸 서비스. 객실로 음식을 직접 가져다 주는 서비스[사람] access one's e-mail 이메일에 접속하다 maintenance 호텔 내의 각종 시설을 보수, 정비하는 「관리부」 send A up …를 올려보내다 wake-up call 모닝콜 heavy sleeper 깊게 잠드는 사람 tip 팁(을 주다). 봉사료 check out 체크아웃하다. 호텔에서 계산을 하고 나가다 concierge 호텔 관리인[안내인] available 이용할 수 있는. 호텔의 경우 「방이 남아 있어 투숙할 수 있는」이란 의미 ~ nights ~박 registration card 숙박계 room rate 객실료

---

3 호텔에서 지내면서

048 I'd like a wake-up call, please

모닝콜 좀 부탁해요

049 A wake-up call, please

모닝콜요

050

What time do you want the call?

몇 시에 전화해드릴까요?

051

I need to be woken up at 6:00 am. I'm a heavy sleeper so you may have to let it ring for a while

아침 6시에 일어나야 해요. 전 깊게 잠들기 때문에 꽤 전화벨을 울려야 할지도 모르겠어요

052

Room service, please

룸서비스 좀 부탁해요

053

Hello. This is room 510. I'd like to order something to eat, but I'm not sure which menu to use

여보세요. 510호실인데요. 식사주문을 하려구요. 그런데 어떤 메뉴판을 보고 골라야 할지 모르겠어요

054

Please bring me a pot of coffee

커피포트 좀 갖다줘요

055

Laundry service, please

세탁서비스 좀 부탁해요

056

Could you recommend a place that will deliver to the hotel?

호텔로 시켜먹을 만한 곳을 추천해주실래요?

057

Antonio's Pizza is really good, the number is 967-1111

앤토니오 피자가 아주 맛있어요. 전화번호는 967–1111입니다

058

I was wondering if you could recommend a restaurant at the hotel

호텔에 있는 식당 좀 추천해주실 수 있을까요?

059

The restaurant on the second floor is well known for its Indian food

2층에 가시면 인도 음식을 잘하는 식당이 있어요

060

I'd like to know how I can access my e-mail

이메일에 접속할 수 있는 방법을 알고 싶은데요

061

Are there any messages for me?

혹 메시지 온 거 있습니까?

062

If you have your own computer you can plug it into the jack beside the phone line

컴퓨터를 가지고 계시면 전화선 옆에 있는 잭에 꽂으시면 됩니다

063

This is room 501. There is no hot water

501호인데 온수가 안 나와요

064

The TV doesn't work in my room

TV가 작동 안돼요

065

I'm calling from room 478 and the air conditioner won't seem to shut off

여긴 478호실인데요. 에어컨이 꺼지질 않아요

066

I pushed the button, but cool air doesn't come out

버튼을 눌렀는데 찬 공기가 안 나와요

067

Could you send someone up?

사람 좀 보내줄래요?

068

Please send someone to help me

사람 좀 보내서 저 좀 도와주세요

069

Could you send someone to fix it?

사람 좀 보내 고쳐줄래요?

070 My room hasn't been cleaned yet

방이 청소가 덜 됐네요

071 I'm afraid the sheets are not clean

시트가 깨끗하지 않아요

072 I locked myself out

문이 잠겨서 못 들어가요

073 I went out without the key, so I'm locked out of my room

열쇠를 두고 나와 방에 못 들어가요

074 I left[forgot] my key inside my room

방에 열쇠를 두고 나왔어요

075 I don't know how to use the card key

이 카드키를 어떻게 사용하는지 모르겠어요

076 I forgot my room number

방번호를 잊었어요

077 I'm lost. I want to go back to room 203

길을 잃었어요. 203호로 가려는데요

078

How much do you think we should tip the cleaning lady?

청소부 팁 얼마 줘야 돼?

079

There is no shampoo in the bath room

욕실에 샴푸가 없어요

080

It's too noisy to sleep in this room

이 방은 자기에 너무 시끄러워요

081

The hot water doesn't come out

온수가 안 나와요

082

Can I control the air conditioning in the room?

방에서 에어컨 조정할 수 있어요?

083

Could you please explain to me about these switches?

이 스위치에 대해 설명해줄래요?

084

The elevator stopped. Help me!

엘리베이터가 멈췄어요. 도와주세요!

085 # What kind of facilities are there in the hotel?

호텔에 어떤 시설들이 있나요?

086 # Could you charge it to my room?

이거 제 방으로 청구해주세요

4 ## 체크아웃 일자 변경

087 # I need to stay another day

하루 더 묵으려고 하는데요

088 # Unfortunately, I need to leave today instead of tomorrow

유감스럽게도 내일이 아니라 오늘 떠나게 되었습니다

089 # My name is Mr. Jung and I was staying in room 307. Unfortunately, I need to leave today instead of tomorrow

이름은 '정'이고 307호에 묵었는데 유감스럽게도 내일이 아니라 오늘 떠나게 되었습니다

090 # It's Mr. Suh in room 301, I need to stay another day

301호의 '서'라고 하는데요, 하루 더 묵으려고 해서요

091 This is Mr. Kim, room 890, and I'd like to check out on the 11th instead of 10th

890호의 김입니다. 10일이 아닌 11일에 체크아웃을 하려합니다

092 I'm Mr. Jung, room 304, and I'd like to stay until 30th instead of 20th

304호의 정인데요 20일 대신 30까지 머물려고요

093 This is Mr. Choi, room 405. I'll be checking out about 10:30. Could you send someone up for my bags?

405호의 최입니다. 10시30분에 체크아웃하려는데 가방 들어 줄 사람 좀 올려주실래요?

094 I'd like to stay two more nights, please

이틀 더 묵을게요

095 Can I stay one more night?

하룻밤 더 묵어도 돼요?

5 체크아웃하면서

096 I'd like to check out now

체크아웃을 하고 싶은데요

097

Check out, please

체크아웃 할게요

098

Could you tell me your room number please?

방 번호를 말씀해 주시겠습니까?

099

I was staying in room 501

501호에 묵었습니다

100

I'm checking out. Room 505, Mr. Jang

체크아웃합니다. 505호실 장입니다

101

Here's your bill

청구서 여기 있습니다

102

I'll get your bill for you

계산서를 갖다 드리겠습니다

103

How would you like to pay for the room, Mr. Kim?

어떻게 지불하고 싶으십니까, 김 선생님?

104

There seems to be some mistake, you have charged me for all four nights

좀 잘못된 게 있는 것 같군요. 4일밤 묵은 걸로 청구하셨네요

105 I'll be paying with traveler's checks

계산은 여행자 수표로 할게요

106 Can I pay for that all on one bill?

나중에 전부 다 한 청구서로 계산할 수 있나요?

107 Please get a taxi for me at 10 am

아침 10시까지 택시불러 주세요

108 I'm checking out. This is the key

체크아웃합니다. 여기 열쇠요

109 I didn't use anything from the refrigerator

냉장고에 있는거 아무 것도 이용하지 않았어요

110 I didn't use the fridge

냉장고 사용하지 않았어요

111 I left something in the room. Can I go back in?

방에 뭔가 두고 왔는데, 들어가도 돼요?

112 What time does the limo leave?

리무진 버스는 몇시에 출발하나요?

COMMON
SENTENCES
IN SITUATION
ENGLISH

113 Is it possible to use a limousine bus to the airport?

공항까지 리무진 버스 이용가능해요?

114 How often does the limousine leave for the airport?

공항가는 리무진 버스는 얼마나 자주 오나요?

115 When does the next limousine leave?

다음 리무진 버스는 언제 출발해요?

116 I had a wonderful time at this hotel, thank you

이 호텔에서 멋진 시간 보냈어요. 고마워요

117 This is a very good hotel

아주 좋은 호텔입니다

118 I like this hotel very much

이 호텔이 정말 좋아요

119 I enjoyed the stay so much

호텔에 머물면서 아주 좋았어요

02 관광

6 관광할 때

120 **Where's the tourist information center?**

관광안내센터가 어디에 있어요?

121 **Can I get a tourist information guide?**

관광정보가이드를 구할 수 있을까요?

122 **May I have a city map?**

시내 지도를 얻을 수 있어요?

123 **Where is the gift shop?**

기념품 점이 어디에 있어요?

124 **Is there a souvenir shop in the hotel?**

호텔에 기념품 점이 있어요?

125 **Please tell me about some interesting places in this town**

시내에 볼만한 곳 좀 알려줘요

126 I was hoping that you could suggest an interesting place close by

주위에 가볼 만한 곳을 권해주셨으면 하는데요

127 What do you recommend for sightseeing?

관광지로 어디를 추천하시겠어요?

128 Do you know any good places to stay[see, eat] in Chicago?

시카고에서 머무를[볼, 먹을] 좋은 곳 알아?

129 What is the best place to visit in this town?

이 마을에서 가장 방문하기 좋은 곳은 어디 인가요?

130 What are your interests?

어디에 관심있어요?

131 Are there any sightseeing buses?

관광버스가 있어요?

132 Is there a sightseeing bus tour?

관광버스투어가 있어요?

133 **What kinds of tours are there?**

어떤 종류의 관광이 있나요?

134 **Tell me about the day trip, please**

당일 여행에 대해 말해주세요

135 **Can I buy a ticket on the day of the tour?**

당일 여행 티켓을 살 수 있을까요?

136 **Which tour returns by five p.m.?**

오후 5시에 돌아오는 관광투어가 어떤 겁니까?

137 **Is there any famous places to visit around here?**

이 근처에 방문할 유명한 곳이 있습니까?

138 **I'd like to join the tour**

그 관광투어를 하고 싶어요

139 **Is there a sightseeing tour bus for the town?**

시내 관광투어버스가 있나요?

140 **What kind of places do we visit on this tour?**

이 투어에서는 어느 곳을 방문하나요?

141 Which is the most popular tour?

가장 인기있는 관광투어가 어떤 건가요?

142 Do you have a night time tour?

밤시간 관광투어가 있나요?

143 Can I find another tour to join now?

지금 할 수 있는 또 다른 투어가 있나요?

144 Can I go to the Niagara Falls in this tour?

이번 투어에서 나이아가라 폭포에 갈 수 있나요?

145 Are meals included in the tour price?

투어비용에 식사가 포함되어 있나요?

146 I'd like a tour by a taxi

택시타고 둘러볼려고요

147 I'd like a guide

가이드가 필요해요

148 I want a Korean-speaking guide

한국말하는 가이드가 필요해요

149

What a beautiful view!

참 멋진 광경이야!

150

Nice place!

멋진 곳이네요!

151

When does the museum open?

박물관은 언제 문 열어요?

152

Are they open on Saturdays?

토요일 날에도 문 여나요?

153

I want to stay longer

더 머물려고요

154

Let's leave now

지금 나가자

155

May I take a picture?

사진 찍어도 돼요?

156

Would you mind posing with me?

저와 사진 찍어도 될까요?

157 Can I take a picture with you?

당신과 사진을 찍어도 될까요?

158 We'd like to take a picture of you and us together. Is it all right?

우리 함께 사진 찍어요? 괜찮겠어요?

159 Can I take a picture of this building?

이 건물 사진 찍어도 되나요?

160 I'd like two tickets for today's game

오늘 게임 표 2장 주세요

161 Two tickets, please

2장요

162 Are there any seats available?

좌석 남아 있나요?

163 Do you have time for shopping?

쇼핑할 시간이 있나요?

164 What does it cost for one person?

일인 당 비용이 어떻게 돼나요?

165 # How late are you open?

언제까지 여나요?

166 # What's the admission charge?

입장료가 얼마인가요?

167 # Where can I see 'Phantom of the Opera?'

어디서 오페라의 유령을 볼 수 있나요?

168 # Where can I get a ticket?

어디서 표를 살 수 있습니까?

169 # I'd like a seat on the first base side

1루석 쪽에 표를 주세요

170 # Is there any good movie showing?

좋은 영화하는 것 있어요?

171 # Is there any movie theater near here?

이 근처에 좋은 극장 있나요?

172 # What kind of movies are showing?

무슨 종류의 영화가 하나요?

173 I prefer some comedies

난 코메디를 좋아해

174 Do you come here often?

여기 자주 오나요?

175 This is my second visit here

여기 두번째 방문예요

176 I'm a tourist

관광객입니다

177 I'm from Korea and this is my second time in Boston

한국에서 왔고 보스톤은 두번 째 방문입니다

178 I'd like to get a hair cut

머리를 깍아주세요

179 Would you like to have a perm?

파마하시겠어요?

180 What are the games for beginners at the Casino?

카지노에서 초보자에게 좋은 게임이 뭐가 있나요?

181
Which is better for a start?

시작하기에 어떤 것이 좋은가요?

182
Slot machine. Put a coin into a slot. That's all

슬롯머신요. 구멍에 코인을 넣기만 하면 돼요

183
Where can I get those chips?

저 칩들은 어디서 살 수 있어요?

184
Cash my chips, please

이 칩을 현금으로 바꿔주세요

✎ **NOTE**

interesting place 흥미로운 곳. 재미있는 곳. 구경할 만한 곳   traveler's check 여행자 수
표   beauty parlor 미장원   admission fee 입장료   ticket office 매표소   fill in 기입하다
intermission (공연)막간   checkroom[cloakroom] 소지품보관소

---

7 관광에서 어려움을 겪을 때

185
My English isn't good enough

영어가 딸려서요

186
I'm a beginner in English, so please go slowly when you talk to me

영어초보여서 말하실 때 천천히 해주세요

187 I don't know how to say it in English

그걸 영어로 어떻게 말하는지 모르겠어요

188 How do you say 'chobop' in English?

초밥을 영어로 뭐라고 하지요?

189 What's 'chobop' in English?

초밥이 영어로 뭐야?

190 What's the English word for 'chobop'?

초밥을 영어로 하면 어떻게 돼?

191 What do you call this in English?

이걸 영어로 뭐라고 해요?

192 Where is the lost and found?

분실물보관소가 어디예요?

193 Call the police! My bag was stolen!

경찰을 불러요! 가방을 도난 당했어요!

194 Is there a police station close by?

근처에 경찰서가 있나요?

195

Who should I report it to?

어디에 신고해야 하죠?

196

I'd like to have a Korean interpreter

한국말 통역하는 사람이 필요해요

197

I need somebody who understands Korean

한국어를 할 줄 아는 사람이 필요해요

198

Does anyone here speak Korean?

여기 누구 한국말 하는 사람 있어요?

199

Where is the Korean Embassy?

한국 대사관이 어디 있어요?

200

I lost my passport

여권을 잃어버렸어요

201

I can't find my passport

여권을 못 찾겠어요

202

I'd like to have my passport reissued

여권을 재발급해주세요

203
I had my purse stolen
지갑을 분실했어요

204
I had my credit card stolen, please cancel it
신용카드를 도난 당했으니 정지시켜주세요

205
Please cancel my credit card
신용카드를 정지시켜주세요

206
I don't remember where I lost it
어디서 잃어버렸는지 기억이 안나요

207
I left my suitcase in the taxi
택시에 가방을 두고 내렸어요

208
Excuse me, but can you make an announcement?
죄송하지만 안내방송 좀 해주시겠어요?

209
My daughter is missing. I'm sure she's in this department
딸을 잃어버렸는데 백화점에 있을거예요

210
Where did you lose her?
따님을 어디서 잃어버렸나요?

211 How old does she look?

인상착의를 말해주세요

212 She has long black hair

머리가 검고 길어요

213 She wears a blue shirt and skirt

파란 셔츠와 치마를 입었어요

8 은행이용하기

214 Where is the currency exchange office?

환전소가 어디입니까?

215 I'd like to change won to dollars, please

원화를 달러로 바꿔주세요

216 Yen to dollars, please

엔화를 달러로 바꿔줘요

217 Could you cash this traveler's check for me?

이 여행자 수표를 현금으로 바꿔줄래요?

218 I'd like to cash this check

이 수표를 현금으로 주세요

219 I'd like to cash my traveler's check

여행자 수표를 현금으로 바꿀려고요

220 Do you have any identification?

신분 증명할거 뭐 있어요?

221 Please fill this out

이걸 작성하세요

222 I'd like to deposit $200

200달러 예금하려고요

223 I'd like to withdraw $100

100달러 인출하려고요

224 I'd like to open an account at your bank

여기 은행에 계좌 하나 만들려고요

225 I'd like to open a savings account

저축계좌 만들려고요

226

I'd like to close my account and withdraw my money

계좌 끝내고 돈 인출해주세요

227

Please endorse it

이서하세요

228

Would you please break this 100 dollar bill for me?

100달러 지폐를 작은 것으로 바꿔줄래요?

229

I'd like this fifty broken into tens

이 50달러를 10달러 지폐로 바꿔줘요

230

Please make it four tens and ten ones

이걸 10달러짜리 4개와 1달러짜리 10개로 바꿔줘요

231

Do you have an account with us?

저희 은행 계좌 갖고 계신가요?

232

I lost my ATM card and need a replacement

카드분실로 재발행해주세요

233 The ATM in your lobby isn't working

로비에 있는 ATM기가 작동안돼요

234 What's the interest rate on my savings account?

저축계좌 이자율은요?

235 What time does your bank open?

은행은 언제 여나요?

Common Sentences
in Situation English

Chapter

04

전화·통신

상황별 영어
대표문장

Common
Sentences
in Situation
English

01 통화

NOTE

operator 전화 교환원   collect call 수신자 부담 전화   local call 시내전화   direct phone
직통전화   area code 지역번호   long distance call 장거리 전화   extension 내선   pay
phone[public telephone] 공중전화

1 통화하고 싶은 사람을 바꿔달라고 할 때

001 Can[May] I speak to Mr. Miller?

밀러 씨 좀 바꿔줄래요?

002 I'd like to speak to the branch manager, please

지사장님 연결해줘요

003 I'm calling to talk to Mr. Kim in the marketing department

마케팅부 김선생님과 통화하려고요

004 Is Mr. Jones there?

존스 씨 계세요?, 존스 씨와 통화하고 싶은데요?

005 Is Mr. Jones in?

존스 씨 계세요?

006 Is Mr. Jones in the office?

존스 씨 사무실에 계세요?

007 Please give me Jane

제인 좀 바꿔주세요

008 Mr. Levine, please

레빈 씨 좀 부탁해요

009 Let me talk to Mr. Levine, please

레빈 씨와 통화할게요

010 Is this the Astron Insurance Company?

애스트론 보험사인가요?

011 Is Mr. Kim available?

김 선생님 계세요?

012 Is Mr. Kim free right now?

김 선생님 지금 통화 돼나요?

013 Is this Mr. Dennis Smith?

데니스 스미스 씨입니까?

014   Is this the billing department?

경리부인가요?

015   Would you put me through to the billing department?

경리부 연결해주실래요?

016   Would you transfer this call to extension 104?

104번으로 돌려줘요

017   Extension 104, please

104번 부탁해요

018   May I have extension 104?

104번 좀 바꿔줄래요?

019   I'd like to get through to Mr. Berkman

버크만 씨 좀 통화하려고요

020   I need to talk to Mr. Harris immediately

해리스 씨와 급히 통화해야 해요

021   It's me

나야

I'd like to speak with …와 통화하고 싶어 May I speak to ~? …를 바꿔주시겠어요? I'm calling to~ …하려고 전화하는거야 transfer A to~ A를 …로 연결시켜주다 leave a message 메시지를 남기다 have A call …에게 전화하라고 하다 call back 다시 전화하다 have a call on the other line 다른 전화가 와있다 get back to …에게 다시 연락하다

2 내가 누구인지 말하고 상대방이 누구인지 물어보기

022
Who's calling please?
누구세요?

023
May I ask who's calling?
누구십니까?

024
Who is this, please?
누구시죠?

025
NTB Company, may I help you?
NTB 회사입니다, 뭘 도와드릴까요?

026
Marketing department
마케팅 부입니다

027
This is James Young
제임스 영이에요

028

This is he

전데요

029

This is

전데요

030

Speaking

전데요

031

It's me, Jane

나야, 제인

032

How may I direct your call?

어디 연결해드릴까요?

033

Who do you want to speak to?

어느 분을 바꿔줄까요?

034

Who would you like to talk to?

어느 분을 바꿔드릴까요?

035

Who are you trying to reach?

어느 분과 통화하실려구요?

036 I'll put you through (right away)

(바로) 바꿔드리죠

037 I'll transfer your call

전화 바꿔드릴게요

038 I'll connect you

연결해 드릴게요

039 I'll get him for you

바꿔드리죠

040 Which Mr. Kim do you want to talk to?

어느 미스터 김과 통화하시겠어요?

041 There are four Kims here

여기에 미스터 김이 4명 있거든요

3 상대방보고 잠시만 기다리라고 할 때

042 Hold on

잠깐만요, 끊지말고 기다려요

043 Hang on

잠시만요

044 Hold the line, please

잠시만요

045 Could you hold?

잠시 기다리실래요?

046 Can you hold the line, please?

잠시만 기다려줄래요?

047 Wait a minute[second]

잠깐만요

048 Just a moment[minute; second], please

잠시만요

049 One moment, please

잠시만요

050 Would you like to hold (on)?

기다리시겠어요?

051 # Sorry to keep you waiting

기다리게 해서 미안해요

052 # I shouldn't have tied you up so long

너무 기다리게 하는 게 아닌데

053 # I've been on hold for a couple of minutes already

벌써 몇분 동안 기다렸어요

4 ## 전화왔다고 말해주기

054 # (There's a) Phone call for you

너한테 전화왔어

055 # You have a phone call

전화왔어요

056 # You've got a call from a friend

한 친구가 전화했어요

057 # You are wanted on the telephone

너한테 전화왔어

058 Some guy just called for you

방금 어떤 사람한테서 전화왔었어

059 I have a call for you

전화왔어

060 You have[There's] a call from Mr. Smith of XYZ Company

XYZ회사의 스미스 씨 전화왔어요

061 Mr. Carter of XYZ is on line 2

2번 라인에 XYZ회사의 카터 씨 전화와 있어요

062 Mr. Carter for you

카터 씨예요

063 It's your girlfriend on the line

여자 친구 전화 와 있어요

064 Excuse me, there's a call on another line

실례지만 다른 전화 와 있어요

 불통

5 전화를 바꿔줄 수 없을 때

065
Her line is busy now
지금 통화 중이신데요

066
(I'm afraid) She's on the other line now
지금 다른 전화 받고 계세요

067
He's talking to someone else now
지금 다른 분과 얘기 중이세요

068
I'm sorry, but he has someone with him right now
미안하지만 지금 손님이 와 계신데요

069
I'm sorry, but she's busy at the moment
미안하지만 지금 바쁘세요

070
I'm sorry, he's not in right now
미안하지만 지금 안에 안 계세요

071
He's in, but he's not at his desk right now
안에 계시는데 지금 자리엔 없네요

072 He's not here now

지금 여기 안 계세요

073 He's out to lunch now

지금 점심 식사하러 나가셨어요

074 He hasn't come back from his lunch yet

아직 점심식사에서 안 돌아오셨어요

075 He's out now

지금 외출 중이에요

076 He's out of the office right now

지금 외근 중이에요

077 He's out on business

출장이에요

078 I'm afraid he's on a business trip

미안하지만 출장 중이신데요

079 He's away on business for a week

일주일 간 출장 중이세요

080 He's out of town now
지금 출장 중이에요

081 He's in a meeting right now
지금 회의 중이세요

082 The advertising department is meeting now
광고부는 지금 회의 중이에요

083 He's off today
오늘 쉬어요

084 When do you expect him back?
언제 돌아오실까요?

085 How soon do you expect him back?
언제쯤 돌아오실까요?

086 When is he coming back?
언제 돌아와요?

087 I'm afraid he's left for the day
오늘 퇴근했어요

088

He won't be back in the office today

오늘 안 돌아오실거예요

089

He should be back in ten minutes

10분내로 돌아올거예요

090

He'll be back in the afternoon

오후에 돌아올거예요

091

Would you like to talk to someone else?

다른 분하고 통화하실래요?

6 전화연결이 안 되어서 메시지를 주고 받을 때

092

Could[May] I leave a message?

메모 좀 전해줄래요?

093

I'd like to leave a message

메모 좀 남길게요

094

Please take a message

메모 좀 남겨주세요

095 ## Could[May] I take a message?

메시지를 전해드릴까요?

096 ## Would you like to leave a message?

메시지를 남기시겠어요?

097 ## Would you tell him that Jim called?

짐이 전화했다고 전해줄래요?

098 ## Do you want him to call you back?

전화하라고 할까요?

099 ## Would you like him to call you back?

전화드리라고 할까요?

100 ## Just have him call me (back)

그냥 전화 좀 해달라고 해주세요

101 ## Please tell[ask] him to call me

내게 전화해달라고 하세요

102 ## Please tell him that I'll call him back

내가 전화 다시 할거라고 전해주세요

103 **I'll tell him that you called**

전화하셨다고 말할게요

104 **I'll have him call you back**

전화드리도록 할게요

105 **I'll tell[ask] him to call you back**

전화드리도록 말할게요

106 **How can I get in touch with him?**

그 사람 연락처가 어떻게 됩니까?

107 **How can he get in contact with you?**

어떻게 당신께 연락드리죠?

108 **Are there any messages?**

메시지 뭐 온 거 있어요?

109 **Do you have any messages?**

메시지 뭐 있어요?

110 **Any messages or phone calls?**

메시지나 전화없었어?

111

Mr. Miller called you during the meeting

밀러 씨가 회의중 전화하셨어요

112

May I have your number?

번호 좀 알려줄래요?

113

Your number, please?

번호 좀요?

114

What's your number?

번호 어떻게 돼요?

115

May I have your name again, please?

성함 좀 다시 말해줄래요?

7 전화가 잘못 걸렸을 때

116

How do you spell your name?

성함 철자 어떻게 쓰나요?

117

Could you please spell your name?

성함 철자 좀 말해줄래요?

118 (I'm afraid) You have the wrong number

전화 잘못 거셨어요

119 You must have the wrong number

전화 잘못 하셨어요

120 I'm sorry, you've got the wrong number

미안하지만 전화 잘못 하셨어요

121 Sorry, wrong number

미안하지만 전화 잘못 걸었어요

122 What number are you calling[dialing]?

어디로 전화하셨어요?

123 What number are you trying to reach?

어느 번호로 전화하신거예요?

124 There's no one here by that name

그런 분 여기 안 계세요

125 There's no Anderson in this office

사무실에 앤더슨이란 사람 없어요

126 There's nobody named Anderson here

여기 앤더슨이란 이름의 사람은 없어요

8 혼선이나 전화 상태가 안 좋을 때

127 I'm sorry, I must have misdialed

죄송해요 전화 잘못 돌렸네요

128 I dialed your number by mistake

다이알을 잘못 돌렸네요

129 I'm sorry, I can't hear you (very well)

죄송하지만 (잘) 안 들려요

130 I'm having trouble hearing you

잘 들리지 않아요

131 Would you speak more slowly, please?

좀 천천히 말씀해주실래요?

132 Could you speak a little louder, please?

좀 크게 말씀해줄래요?

133 **Could you repeat that?**

다시 한번 말해줄래요?

134 **We have a bad connection**

혼선이야

135 **You sound very far away**

감이 아주 멀어

136 **There's noise on my line**

내 전화선에 소음이 있어

137 **Let me call you from another line**

다른 선으로 전화할게

138 **Could you dial again?**

다시 걸래요?

139 **The phone went dead**

전화가 죽었어

140 **I was cut off**

전화가 끊겼어

상황별 영어
대표문장

MON
TENCES
ITUATION
KISH

03 전화끊기

NOTE

make[place] an overseas call 국제 전화를 하다 be connected 전화가 연결되다 hold (전화를 끊지 않고) 기다리다 have A on the line A로부터 전화가 와 있다 answer the phone 전화를 받다 be set to vibrate (휴대폰을) 진동으로 해놓다 text message 문자 메시지 person-to-person call 지명 통화 전화

9 다음에 통화하자고 하면서 전화를 끊을 때

141

I have to go now

전화 그만 끊어야겠어

142

I've got to go

그만 끊을게

143

It's been good talking to you

통화해서 좋았어요

144

I'm sorry, I can't talk long

미안하지만 길게 얘긴 못해

145

(I'll) Talk to you soon

또 걸게, 다음에 통화하자

146

Talk to you tomorrow

내일 얘기하자

147 Could you call back later?

나중에 전화할래?

148 Would you mind calling back later?

나중에 전화해도 돼?

149 Would you call again later?

나중에 전화할래요?

150 Please call me back in ten minutes

10분 후에 전화 줘

151 Please call again anytime

아무 때나 전화 다시 해

152 I'll call back later

나중에 전화할게

153 I'll call you again

다시 전화할게

154 I'll catch up with you later

나중에 연락할게

155 Get back to me

나중에 연락해

156 I'll get back to you when you're not so busy

너 안 바쁠 때 다시 전화할게

157 Could I call you?

나중에 전화해도 될까요?

158 Would you please get off the phone?

전화 좀 끊을테야?

159 Give me a call[ring; buzz]

전화해

160 Thank you[Thanks] for calling

전화줘서 고마워

161 Thank you for your call

전화줘서 고마워

162 Thank you for returning my call

전화걸어줘서 고마워

10 핸드폰 영어표현

163

I'm sorry, but my phone was set to vibrate

미안해요, 진동으로 했놓았거든요

164

I always have my phone on vibrate

난 핸드폰 항상 진동으로 해놔

165

My cell phone is on silent mode

내 휴대폰은 진동으로 해놨어

166

Did you see that I sent you a text message?

제가 보낸 문자 받았어?

167

I'll send it to you in a text message

문자메시지로 보내줄게

168

I'm calling you because I saw that you called me

부재중 전화가 와서 전화하는거야

169

The first name on my speed number is you

스피드 단축번호의 첫 번째 이름은 너야

170

Call me on your cell phone

핸드폰으로 전화해

171

She's on a cell phone

핸드폰으로 통화중이야

172

Why didn't you answer your cell phone?

왜 핸드폰 안 받았어?

173

I forgot it at home today

집에 놔두고 왔어

174

I turned my cell phone off

핸드폰 꺼놨어

175

You're breaking up

소리가 끊겨

176

My cell phone isn't getting good reception

내 핸드폰 수신상태가 안 좋아

177

We get bad reception in the elevator

엘리베이터에서는 수신상태가 안 좋아

178 I've been calling your cell phone
네 핸드폰으로 계속 전화했어

179 My battery went dead and it stopped working
배터리가 죽어서 작동이 안돼

180 My battery is dying
배터리가 다해서 끊어지려고 해

181 You'd better keep your cell phone charged
핸드폰 충전해놓고 다녀

182 Is your cell phone not working?
핸드폰 안돼?

183 Your cell phone is ringing
너 핸드폰 온다

184 I like your ring tone
벨소리 좋네

185 Do you mind if I answer this call?
이 전화 받아도 돼요?

상황별 영어
대표문장

SES
ION

05 기타

11 전화영어에 자주 쓰이는 표현들

186
I'm sorry for calling you this late
너무 늦게 전화해서 미안해

187
Am I calling too late?
내가 너무 늦게 전화했니?

Chapter 04

188
I hope I'm not disturbing you
방해한게 아니었으면 해

189
I'm calling to ask you for a favor
도움 좀 청할려고 전화했어

190
I'm calling about tomorrow's meeting
내일 회의 문제로 전화한거야

191
Excuse me, is there someone there who can speak Korean?
실례지만, 한국어하는 사람 있어요?

192
Are you (still) there?
듣고 있는 거니?, 여보세요?

193 I called, but your line was busy

전화했는데 통화 중이더라

194 I was expecting your call

네 전화 기다리고 있었어

195 He's expecting your call

당신 전화를 기다리고 있었어요

196 Where can I reach him?

어떻게 그 사람에게 연락하죠?

197 You can reach me at 010-3794-5450 until six o'clock

6시까진 010-3794-5450으로 하세요

198 Hello, I got your message on my answering machine

여보세요, 응답기에 메시지가 있어서

199 I heard you called this morning

오늘 아침 전화했다고 들었어요

200

You called?

전화하셨어요?

201

I'm sorry I wasn't in when you called

전화했을 때 자리 비워서 미안해요

202

I'm returning your call

전화했다고 해서 하는거야

203

I'm sorry I didn't get back to you sooner

더 빨리 연락 못 줘서 미안해

204

Hello, this is Mr. Fick and I'm returning Mr. Kim's call

픽예요, 김선생이 전화했다고 해서요

205

I'm sorry I've taken so much of your time

너무 오래 붙잡고 있었네요

206

He won't take my calls

걘 내 전화를 안 받으려고 해

207

Give me a call

전화해

208 I've been meaning to call you

안그래도 전화하려고 했어

209 I have got another call

다른 전화가 왔어

210 I'm getting another call

다른 전화가 오고 있는데

 이메일

12 이메일 주고 받을 때

211 **Let's meet there at the chat room at 9:00**

9시에 채팅방에서 만나자

212 **I found your ad on the web and would like to be friends**

인터넷에서 광고를 봤는데 친구하고 싶어서요

213 **I'm afraid I sent my e-mail to the wrong address**

다른 주소로 이메일을 보낸 것 같아

214 **Please give me your e-mail address**

이메일 주소 좀 알려줘

215 **Can you give me her e-mail address?**

걔 이메일 주소 좀 알려줄래?

216 **My e-mail address is ENC@gmail.com**

내 이메일 주소는 ENC@gmail.com이야

217

You can e-mail me at ENC@gmail.com

ENC@gmail.com으로 메일 보내

218

I'll let you know my new e-mail address as soon as I get it

내가 이메일 만들면 바로 새 이메일주소 알려줄게

219

I have a new e-mail address because I've changed my Internet service providers

인터넷 업체를 바꿔서 이메일 주소가 바뀌었어

220

My e-mail address has been changed to ENC@gmail.com

바뀐 내 이메일 주소는 ENC@gmail.com이야

221

Please change my address ABC@gmail.com to ENC@gmail.com

내 이메일 주소를 ABC@gmail.com에서 ENC@gmail.com으로 바꾸라고

222

Do e-mail me when you get a chance

시간되면 이메일보내

223

Thank you for your e-mail of March 17

3월 17일자 이메일 고마워

224

I'll e-mail you later

나중에 이메일 보낼게

225

I will send you e-mail again

다시 이메일 보낼게

226

I received your e-mail of June 21

6월 21일 보낸 이메일 받았어

227

I'm writing with regard to your e-mail of May 12

보내신 5월 12일자 이메일 건으로 글을 씁니다

228

I still haven't received any e-mail from you

네게서 아직 아무런 이메일도 못 받았어

229

Wishing you a very Merry Christmas and the happiest of New Years

즐거운 성탄절을 맞고 행복한 새해를 맞기를 바래

230

Best wishes for a Happy Holiday Seasons and much happiness in the New Year

즐거운 휴일보내고 새해엔 복 많이 받기를 바래

231

Wishing you a beautiful Holiday Season and a Happy New Year

휴일 멋지게 보내고 새해 복 많이 받아

232

Please delete my name from your mailing list

귀사의 발송자 명단에서 절 빼주세요

233

I just wanted to drop you an e-mail to say 'hi'

그냥 인사나 하려고 이메일보냈어

234

I would like to take this opportunity to thank you for your kindness and hospitality

이 기회를 빌어 당신의 친절과 호의에 감사드립니다

235

I'm sending a quick e-mail to let you know that I'll be arriving this Sunday

이번 일요일날 도착한다고 알려주려고 짧게 이메일 보내는거야

236

Please forward my e-mail to my new address

내 이메일을 새로운 주소로 전송해줘

237

I'll be waiting to hear from you

연락기다리고 있을게

238 Write back when you can

시간되면 연락해

239 Please write me whenever you can

언제든 시간되면 연락해

240 I'm looking forward to hearing from you soon

소식 주기를 학수고대하고 있겠습니다

241 I'm looking forward to your early reply

빨리 답장 주기를 기다릴게요

242 We look forward to your prompt response

빠른 답신을 기다립니다

243 Please return e-mail ASAP

가능한한 빨리 이메일 답줘

244 I still haven't received a response from you

아직 너로부터 답장을 못 받았어

245 Thank you for your quick response

빨리 답장줘서 고마워

246 Thank you for your response to my e-mail of October 25

내 10월 25일자 이메일에 답장을 해줘서 고마워요

247 Thank you so much for your prompt reply to my e-mail of January 11

내 1월 11일자 이메일에 바로 답을 줘서 무척 고마워요

248 I sent a reply to you

답장 보냈어

249 I'm sorry I didn't reply to you sooner

빨리 답신을 못해서 미안해요

250 Sorry for not responding earlier

좀 더 일찍 답을 못줘 미안해

251 I'm sorry I haven't had time to write earlier, but I've been so busy

좀 더 일찍 소식 못 전해 미안하지만 정말 바빴어

252 It has taken me so long to respond to you. As you probably know, I'm busy

답장 쓰는데 시간이 너무 걸렸네. 아마 알다시피, 내가 바빠서

253
Attached please find a detailed statement

상세한 명세서를 첨부했습니다

254
I'm attaching a file to this e-mail

이 이메일에 파일을 첨부했어

255
Thank you for your time and thank you for reading this e-mail

시간내줘서 그리고 이 이메일을 읽어주셔서 감사합니다

256
I can't read the attached file

첨부파일을 읽지 못하겠어

257
I was unable to log on to the computer

컴퓨터에 로그인이 안됐어

258
I couldn't get this file to open. It reads 'error reading file.' I downloaded it several times, but the result was the same

파일이 열리지가 않아. "파일읽기에러"라고 적혀있어. 여러 번 다운로드했는데 마찬가지야

259 I got both of your e-mails and tried to download both files, but neither would download again. I'm not sure what the problem is, because other files that have been sent download OK

네가 보내준 메일 2개를 받았는데 다운로드가 안돼. 문제가 뭔지 모르겠어. 다른 첨부 파일 들은 다운로드 잘 되거든

260 Let's try sending it to my yahoo e-mail: ENC@yahoo.com. It may be a problem that is specific to hotmail. If that doesn't work, we can cut and paste the file again

내 야후 이메일인 ENC@yahoo.com으로 보내봐. 핫메일만의 문제일 수도 있거든. 그래도 안되면 텍스트를 잘라 붙여 보내자

261 For some reason the attachment wouldn't open. Could you send the general contents within an e-mail?

어떤 이유에선가 첨부파일이 열리지 않아. 이메일에 텍스트로 보내줄래?

262 I'm sorry for not answering sooner. For some reason, there was a problem accessing my hotmail account the last few times I used the Internet

더 빨리 답 못해 미안. 어떤 이유에선가 인터넷을 하는데 핫메일 계정이 열리지 않았어

263 Have you gotten any of my e-mails? I sent several but they have been returned to me saying the message delivery was delayed. I'm not sure if any got through to you

내가 보낸 이메일 받아봤어? 여러 번 보냈는데 발송이 지연되었다는 메시지와 함께 되돌아 와. 네가 받은게 있는지 모르겠네

264 I got a notification that the e-mail I sent you had been delayed, so I'm sending it again

내가 보낸 이메일이 지연되었다고 해서 다시 보내는 거야

265 I am sorry I did not send it sooner. I am traveling in Paris this week, and it has been difficult to find Internet access

더 빨리 보내지 못해 미안. 이번 주에 파리 여행을 하고 있어 인터넷이 되는 곳을 찾기가 어려웠어

266 I just got home from a trip Montreal tonight and saw your e-mail. Unfortunately, there was no chance to check e-mail when I was traveling in Canada

오늘 밤에 몬트리올에서 집에 돌아와 네 메일을 봤어. 안타깝게도 캐나다를 여행하면서 네 메일을 확인할 기회가 없었어

267 Starting on Sunday, I have tried to send this to you 4 times, and I'm not sure why it keeps getting rejected. Anyhow, hopefully it will reach you through your other e-mail address

일요일부터 이걸 보내려고 4번이나 해봤는데 왜 거절되어 오는지 모르겠어. 어쨌거나 네 다른 이메일 주소로 받아볼 수 있기를 바래

268 They went to my junk e-mail instead of my regular inbox

이메일들이 받은메일함이 아니라 스팸메일박스로 갔어

269 It seems like your ENC@nate.com account is working OK now. I haven't had any messages returned from it lately

네 ENC@nate.com 계정은 잘 되는 것 같아. 최근엔 반송되는게 없었어

270 I'm glad the files have gotten through to you. I've been sending to both of your e-mail addresses, but lately, most of the files to ENC@gmail.com seem to be getting returned. I guess the ENC@yahoo.com address is working well

파일들을 네가 받아봤다니 다행야. 네 계정 두 곳으로 보냈는데 ENC@gmail.com은 계속 반송되는 것 같아. ENC@yahoo.com이 잘 되는 것 같아

271 I tried to send you this e-mail a few days ago but it keeps returning to my inbox. Please let me know if it gets to you

몇일 전에 이 이메일을 보내려고 했는데 내 받은메일함으로 자꾸 돌아와. 혹시 받았으면 알려줘

272 I didn't get an e-mail from you, so I'm not sure if you received these files when I resent them to you yesterday. Anyhow, this is the third time I'm sending them, so I hope they get through to you

너한테서 이메일이 오지 않아 어제 내가 다시 보낸 이 파일들을 네가 받았는지 모르겠어. 어쨌든 3번째 이것들을 보내는데 네게 도착하기를 바래

273 I just sent you a file. Please check to see that you got it

방금파일을 보냈는데 제대로 받았는지 확인해봐

274 I just wanted to confirm that I got your file today and will be working on it

오늘 네 파일 받아서 작업하고 있다는 걸 알려주려고

275 I didn't get back until very late Sunday night, and couldn't check e-mail until yesterday

일요일 저녁 늦게서야 도착했고 어제야 이메일을 확인할 수 있었어

문자·메신저

13 문자나 메신저를 주고 받을 때

276

Just add your new friend to your Messenger list

네 메신저에 새로운 친구를 추가하면 돼

add sb to one's Messenger list …의 메신저에 …을 추가하다

277

Students use instant messenger for discussing homework

학생들은 과제물을 토의하는데 메신저를 이용해

use instant messenger for …하는데 메신저를 사용하다

278

Sam sent an instant message to her boyfriend

샘은 자기 남친에게 IM을 보냈어

send an instant messenger to sb …에게 IM을 보내다

279

My sister IMed me about a concert tomorrow night

누이는 내일밤 콘서트에 관해 내게 메신저를 보냈어

S+IMed sb about~ …에 관해 …에게 IM을 보냈다

280

Do you think he'll tweet about his trip overseas?

걔가 자기 해외여행에 관해 트위터에 올릴 것 같아?

tweet (about) sth 트위터에 (…에 관해) 올리다

281
Ray is in his bedroom updating his Facebook page

레이는 침대에서 자신의 페이스북 페이지를 업데이트하고 있어

update one's Facebook 자신의 페이스북을 업데이트하다

282
Some people find old classmates on Facebook

페이스북에서는 옛날 동창들을 찾는 사람들도 있어

find sb on Facebook 페이스북에서 …을 찾다

283
After she was bullied, Jen decided to delete her Facebook account

젠은 괴롭힘을 당한 후에 페이스북 계정을 삭제하기로 했어

delete one's Facebook account 페이스북 계정을 삭제하다

284
It was a great vacation, and I'm going to facebook the experience

정말 멋진 여행였어, 경험한 것들을 페이스북에 올릴거야.

facebook 페이스북하다, 페이스북으로 연락하다

285
We're just waiting for her to send us a text message

우리는 걔가 우리에게 문자 보내기를 기다리고 있어

send sb a text message …에게 문자메시지를 보내다

286
Alex got a text message saying his mom is in the hospital

알렉스는 엄마가 병원에 계시다는 문자를 받았어

get a text message saying~ …라는 문자메시지를 받다

287
You'd better text message them to say we'll be late

넌 걔네들에게 문자를 보내 우리가 늦을거라고 말해

text message sb …에게 문자메시지를 보내다

288
On our date, she kept texting her ex-boyfriend

데이트하는데 그녀는 계속해서 옛 남친에게 문자를 보냈어

text sb …에게 문자를 보내다

289
You need to login to Facebook to check her status

걔가 어떻게 지내는지 확인하려면 페이스북에 로그인해야 돼

login to Facebook 페이스북에 로그인하다 *Facebook status는 일상에 있었던 일들을 올려 놓은 상태를 말한다.

290
Several people liked the tweet about our festival

몇몇 사람들이 우리 축제에 관한 트윗을 좋아한다고 표시했어

"Like" a tweet 트윗의 내용이 좋다고 표시하다

291
Is there a way for me to link to Tracey's Facebook page?

내가 트레이시의 페이스북에 연결하는 방법이 있어?

link to a Facebook page 페이스북에 연결하다

292
They are going to be live streaming the conference

그들은 회의를 실시간으로 중계할거야

be live streaming 인터넷으로 생중계하다

Chapter

05

음식·식당

COMMON
SENTENCES
IN SITUATION
ENGLISH

상황별 영어
대표문장

01 식당

delicatessen 델리카트센, 조제(調劑) 식품점 automat 간이식당 cafeteria 카페테리아 ethnic restaurant 민속음식점 lunch counter 간이식당 today's special 오늘의 요리 seasoning 조미료, 양념 condiments 조미료 flavored 맛을 낸, 맛이 있는 table d'hote 정식 delicious 음식이 맛있는 hot 뜨거운, 톡쏘는 salty 짠 spicy 향료를 넣은, 매운(hot) sour 시큼한, 신 bitter 쓴

001 Is there a good restaurant?

좋은 식당이 있나요?

002 Is there a Korean restaurant close by?

근처에 한국 식당이 있습니까?

003 Where is the closest Korean restaurant?

가장 가까운 한국식당이 어디예요?

004 Which restaurant do you recommend?

어느 식당을 추천해주실래요?

005 Can you recommend a good restaurant for local food?

이 지역 음식을 먹을 좋은 식당을 추천해주실래요?

006
Which is the closest Japanese restaurant from here?

여기서 가장 가까운 일본 식당이 어느 곳인가요?

007
Could you recommend a good restaurant near here?

근처에 좋은 식당 추천해줄래요?

008
Is there a Mexican restaurant around here?

이 근처에 멕시코 식당 있나요?

Chapter 05

009
Are there any restaurants still open near here?

근처에 아직 문 연 식당 있나요?

010
I'd like to take her out for dinner on the weekend

주말에 걔 데리고 가서 저녁먹고 싶어

011
I'd like to take you to try some Italian food

널 데리고 가서 이태리음식 맛보자

012
Would you like to join us for some cocktails?

함께 칵테일 좀 마실테야?

013 Is this a self service restaurant?

셀프서비스 식당인가요?

2 예약없이 식당가기

014 I didn't make a reservation. Can I get a seat?

예약을 안 했는데 자리 있나요?

015 Is there a table available?

자리 있어요?

016 Can I take this seat?

이 자리에 앉아도 돼요?

017 All the seats are taken right now

모든 자리가 다 찼어요

018 No tables are available now

앉을 자리가 없는데요

019 How long do we have to wait for a table?

자리나려면 얼마나 기다려야 하나요?

020 What time can I get a table?

언제 자리가 나죠?

021 How long is the wait?

얼마나 기다려야 하나요?

022 How long do we have to wait?

얼마동안 기다려야 합니까?

023 Is the wait long?

오래 기다려야 합니까?

Chapter 05

024 I'll be in the bar until I can get a seat

자리 날 때까지 바에 있죠

025 I've been waiting for 30 minutes

30분간 기다렸는데요

026 We'd like to have seats together, please

함께 앉을 자리를 주세요

3 식당 예약하기

027

Do I need a reservation?

예약이 필요합니까?

028

Is it necessary to make a reservation?

예약을 해야 하나요?

029

I'd like to reserve a table for seven

일곱 명 예약하고 싶은데요

030

What time can we make a reservation for?

몇시에 예약할 수 있나요?

031

I'd like to make a reservation for four tonight

오늘밤 4명 예약하려구요

032

I'd like to make a reservation for 6 o'clock

6시에 예약할게요

033

I'd like to make a reservation for tonight

오늘밤에 예약할게요

034

All the tables are reserved for that time

그 시간에는 예약이 다 찼습니다

035 After eight will be fine
8시 이후에는 괜찮습니다

036 How many of you, sir?
몇분이십니까?

037 For how many people?
몇명이세요?

038 Three persons at 7 p.m.
7시에 3명입니다

039 Would you like a table by the window?
창가자리를 원하세요?

040 I'd like to reserve a table near the window
창가에 예약하고 싶어요

041 I'd like to get a table in the corner
구석자리를 주세요

042 Would you like smoking or nonsmoking?
흡연석 아니면 금연석으로요?

043 ## I'd like to have a non-smoking seat

비흡연석으로 주세요

044 ## I'm sorry. We're all booked up tonight

미안하지만 오늘밤은 예약 다 끝났어요

045 ## I'm sorry. We're quite full tonight

미안하지만 오늘밤은 다 찼습니다

046 ## I'm sorry, but I have to cancel my reservation

죄송하지만 예약 취소해야 될 것 같아서요

047 ## Please cancel my reservation for tonight

오늘밤 예약 취소해주세요

상황별 영어
대표문장

ES
ION

음식

4 어떤 음식을 먹을지 물어보기

048 ### What would you like (to have)?
뭘 드시겠어요?

049 ### What will you have?
뭘 할래요?

050 ### What are you going to have?
뭘 들래?

051 ### What are you having?
넌 뭐 먹을래?

052 ### What's yours?
네거는 뭔데?, 즐겨 마시는게 뭔데?

053 ### What would you like to have for an appetizer?
애피타이저로 뭘 할래요?

054 ### What would you like to have for dinner this evening?
오늘밤 저녁식사로 뭐 할래요?

055 What do you want to eat for lunch today?

오늘 점심 뭐 먹을래?

056 What's your favorite food?

어떤 음식을 좋아하세요?

057 I'd like to have some seafood

해산물을 먹고 싶어요

058 Is there any special dish that you like?

뭐 특별히 좋아하는 음식 있어?

059 Which do you prefer to have, Italian or Mexican food?

이태리 아니면 멕시코 음식이 좋아?

060 Would you like some coffee?

커피 좀 들래요?

061 Would you care for some coffee?

커피 좀 들래요?

062 How about some coffee?

커피 어때?

063
Let's have a light meal
간단한 식사로 하자

064
I don't care for heavy foods
배불리 먹는 건 싫어

065
I don't have any strong likes or dislikes
특별히 좋아하거나 싫어하는 거 없어

066
Sushi is my favorite dish
스시는 내가 가장 좋아하는 음식이야

067
Raw fish is my least favorite food
날 생선은 내가 가장 좋아하지 않은 음식이야

068
I'm sick of hamburgers
햄버거는 싫증나

069
I don't have much of an appetite
식욕이 별로 없어

NOTE

grilled salmon 그릴 새우   fried prawns 새우튀김   abalone 전복   clam 대합   cod 대구
crab 게   crawfish 가재   escargot 달팽이   herring 청어   lobster 바닷가재   shrimp 새우
mackerel 고등어   mussel 홍합   octopus 문어   squid 오징어   oyster 굴   plaice 가자미
prawn 참새우(크기는 lobster와 shrimp 사이)   salmon 연어   trout 송어   salmon roe 훈제연어
알   sardine 정어리   scallop 가리비   sea bass 농어   sea urchin 성게   swordfish 황새치
tuna 참치

5 식당에서 손님에게 음식 주문을 주고 받을 때

070

Are you ready to order?

주문하시겠어요?

071

Are you ready for dessert?

디저트 준비하시겠어요?

072

May I take your order?

주문 받을까요?

073

What's your order?

뭘 주문하시겠습니까?

074

What would you like to order?

뭘 주문하시겠습니까?

075

Which dressing would you like with your salad?

샐러드에 무슨 드레싱을 해드릴까요?

076 We'll wait. Please call us when you're ready

기다리겠습니다. 준비되시면 부르세요

077 What can I get you, sir?

뭘 갖다 드릴까요, 손님?

078 What'll it be?

뭘로 드시겠어요?

079 Would you care for dessert?

디저트 드시겠어요?

080 Have you chosen your dessert?

디저트를 고르셨나요?

081 How would you like your steak?

스테이크를 어떻게 해드릴까요?

082 How would you like your steak cooked [prepared]?

스테이크를 어떻게 해드릴까요?

083 How would you like it done?

그걸 어떻게 해드릴까요?

084 How do you like your coffee?

커피 어떻게 해드릴까요?

085 What do you take in your coffee?

커피에 뭘 넣으시나요?

086 Would you care for a glass of wine with your dinner?

저녁식사에 와인 한 잔 할래요?

087 Is that all?

그게 전부입니까?

088 Would you like to order something else, or will that be all?

다른 주문하실래요 아님 다 됐나요?

089 Is there anything else you'd like?

다른 거 뭐 더 필요한거는요?

090 Anything else?

다른 건요?

091

Anything else you want?

다른 거 더 필요한 건요?

092

That's all (for me)

(전) 됐어요

093

That's it

됐어요

094

That will be all

그게 다예요

095

My order[dishes] hasn't come yet

주문이 아직 안 나왔어요

096

We're still waiting for our food

아직 음식이 안 나왔어요

097

This is not what I ordered

내가 주문한 게 아닌데요

098

I didn't order this

이거 주문 안 했는데요

099 I'm sorry, but I ordered something different

죄송하지만 다른 걸 주문했는데요

100 I don't think I ordered this

이거 주문 안 했는데요

101 I ordered 3 cups of coffee. But we only got two

커피 3잔 주문했는데 2잔만 나왔어요

102 Which would you like to have, coffee or tea?

커피를 드시겠어요 아니면 차를 드시겠어요?

103 This glass is not very clean

이 잔이 깨끗하지 않은데요

104 Can I cancel my order, please?

주문 취소해도 돼요?

105 I have to leave soon. Could you please hurry up?

곧 나가야 하는데 서둘러줄래요?

106 Could you hurry with our orders?

음식 아직 멀었어요?

107 Will it take much longer?

시간이 많이 걸리나요?

108 Would you rush my order?

주문 좀 서둘러줄래요?

109 I think you can have it soon

곧 나옵니다

110 We'll bring your order right up

주문하신 것 바로 가져다 드릴게요

NOTE

vegetable 야채 asparagus 아스파라거스 bean 콩 broccoli 브로콜리 cabbage 양배추 carrot 당근 celery 셀러리 corn 옥수수 cucumber 오이 eggplant 가지 green pepper 피망 kidney bean 강낭콩 olive 올리브 lettuce 상추, 양상추 onion 양파 parsley 파슬리 pickeles 절인야채 (특히 오이) potato 감자 pumpkin 호박 spinach 시금치 sweet potato 고구마 tomato 토마토 beverage 음료 cream puff 슈크림빵 parfait 아이스크림과 케익중간 sherbet 셔벗(과즙 아이스크림) souffle 아주 부드러운 케익 tart 타트(과일 등을 얹은 작은 파이) pudding 푸딩(밀가루에 달걀, 우유, 과일, 설탕, 향료를 넣고 구운 식후용 과자) cereal 시리얼 '아침식사용 곡물 confectionary 과자의, 사탕의 croissant 크루아상(초승달 모양의 롤빵) muffin 머핀(옥수수 가루 따위를 넣어서 살짝 구운 빵) shortcake 네모난 과일 케이크 whipped cream 거품 크림 club sandwich 클럽샌드위치(찬 고기나 샐러드 등을 끼워 넣은 3겹 샌드위치) roll 롤빵

6 음식을 선택하기

111 I'd like to see a menu, please

메뉴 좀 갖다주세요

112 Could[May] I have a menu, please?

메뉴 좀 보여주세요

113 Can I see the menu again?

메뉴 좀 다시 보여주세요

114 Can I order now?

지금 주문해도 돼요?

115 Can I have only coffee?

커피만 마셔도 돼요?

116 Do you have a set menu?

세트메뉴 있어요?

117 Do you have a dessert menu?

디저트 메뉴 있어요?

118 What do you suggest[recommend]?

당신은 뭘 권하시겠어요?

119 What would you recommend[suggest] as an appetizer?

애피타이저로 뭘 추천해줄래요?

120 What would you recommend[suggest] for
dessert?

디저트로 뭘 추천해줄래요?

121 Can you tell me what's good here?

이 곳은 어떤 요리가 괜찮은지 말씀해 주시겠어요?

122 What do you think I should order?

뭘 주문해야 될까요?

123 What do you think is the best?

뭐가 가장 좋은 것 같아요?

Chapter 05

124 What kind of wine do you have?

와인은 무슨 종류가 있어요?

125 May I see the wine list, please?

와인리스트 좀 볼 수 있을까요?

126 What kind of dressing do you have?

드레싱으로론 뭐가 있어요?

127 What kind of salad do you have?

어떤 샐러드가 있나요?

128 What is the special of the day?

오늘의 스페셜은 뭔가요?

129 Can you tell me about the specials of the day?

오늘 스페셜이 뭐예요?

130 What is tonight's special?

오늘 스페셜이 뭐예요?

131 Look, I don't speak English well. Just let me have Today's special

저기요 영어가 달려서요. 그냥 오늘의 스페셜로 주세요

132 Do you have any local specialties?

이 지역 특산물이 있어요?

133 I can recommend the cheesecake. It's excellent

치즈스테이크가 아주 좋습니다

134 I'd recommend the nachos with hot peppers

후추를 곁들인 나초를 권해드릴게요

135

I'd suggest the chicken wings to go with your beer

맥주엔 닭날개를 드세요

136

What comes with that?

함께 뭐가 나오나요?

137

Does it come with soup or salad and dessert?

수프나 샐러드, 디저트가 함께 나오나요?

138

Is coffee included with this meal?

식사에 커피가 포함되어 있나요?

139

What is that like?

그거 어떤 거예요?

140

What kind of dish is this?

이건 어떤 음식인가요?

141

I haven't made up my mind yet

아직 결정을 못했는데요

142

Does it contain any alcohol?

알코올이 들어있나요?

143 **Do they contain any additives?**

첨가물이 뭐 들어 있나요?

144 **May I have another glass of water?**

물 한 잔 더 주세요

145 **Can I order wine by the glass?**

잔으로 와인 주문돼요?

146 **Please recommend a good wine for the dish?**

음식에 맞는 좋은 와인 좀 추천해줘요

147 **Can you please change my order?**

주문 좀 바꿔줄래요?

148 **Can you please take this away?**

이것 좀 치워줄래요?

149 **I'd like to have some more bread, please**

빵 좀 더 주세요

150 **Excuse me, I dropped my knife**

죄종하지만 칼을 떨어트렸네요

151 Hamburger and Cola, take out, please

햄버거하고 콜라 포장해주세요

152 Small, medium or large size?

작은 거, 중간, 아니면 큰 걸로요?

153 Small hot dog and large Cola

작은 핫도그와 큰 콜라주세요

154 Is that all?

그게 전부인가요?

155 I'd like to have a light meal

가벼운 식사하려구요

156 How do I eat this?

이거 어떻게 먹어요?

157 No pickles with the hamburger, please

햄버거에 피클은 빼주세요

158 I want lots of ketchup

케첩을 많이 넣어주세요

159 ## No mustard, please

겨자는 넣지 마세요

7 음식을 선택해서 달라고 할 때

160 ## I'll have the same

같은 걸로 주세요

161 ## Can I have the same as him?

저 사람과 같은 걸로 줄래요?

162 ## The same for me

나도 같은 걸로요

163 ## I'd like to have the same dish as the next table

옆 테이블과 같은 걸로 주세요

164 ## Make it two

같은 걸로 2개 주세요

165 ## I'll have that

그걸로 주세요

I'll take this one

이걸로 주세요

167

I'll take this and this

이거하고 이거 먹을게요

168

I'd like a steak

고기 먹을래요

169

I'd like some Italian food

이태리 음식 좀 주세요

Chapter **05**

170

I'd like a hamburger and an ice tea

햄버거하고 아이스티 주세요

171

I'd like to try the steak

고기를 먹어보죠

172

I'd like something to drink

마실 것 좀 주세요

173

I'd like some more wine

와인 좀 더 주세요

174 I'd like a cup of coffee, please

커피 한잔 주세요

175 I'd like another cup of coffee

커피 한잔 더 주세요

176 I'll have a chocolate muffin

초코렛 머핀으로 주세요

177 I'll have the chocolate mousse and my wife will have the cheesecake

전 초콜릿 무스, 아낸 치즈케익으로 줘요

178 Can I get a steak sandwich and a Coke?

고기샌드위치랑 콜라 하나 줄래요?

179 Can you get me a glass of water, please?

물 한잔 갖다 줄래요?

180 May I have two hot dogs, please?

핫도그 두 개 주실래요?

181 I'd like my steak medium

고기는 미디엄으로 해주세요

182 Well-done, please

웰던으로 해줘요

183 No dessert, thank you. Just coffee, please

디저트는 됐구요, 그냥 커피주세요

184 Please give me a low calorie sugar, please

저칼로리 설탕주세요

chef's specialty 주방장 특별요리　pasta 파스타(달걀을 섞은 가루 반죽을 재료로 한 이탈리아 요리)　made-to-order food 주문(해 만든 요리)　cold cuts 가공육(얇게 저민 냉육과 치즈로 만든 요리) filling (음식물의) 속, 내용물　topping (음식물위에) 얹은 것　whipping cream 거품이 일기에 알맞은 크림　fat-free 지방을 뺀

8 음식 권하기

185 Help yourself

마음껏 드세요, 어서 갖다 드세요

186 Help yourself to some cheese and crackers

치즈하고 크래커 갖다 드세요

187 Help yourself to anything (in the refrigerator)

(냉장고에 있는 거) 마음껏 드세요

188 Help yourself to whatever you like

원하는 거 아무거나 갖다 드세요

189 Enjoy your meal

맛있게 드세요

190 What's for dinner?

저녁식사 메뉴가 뭐야?

191 Is dinner ready?

저녁 됐어?

192 Today, we're having curry

오늘은 카레라이스야

193 Come and get it

자 와서 먹자, 자 밥 먹게 와라

194 Please feel free to have another

어서 더 들어요

195 Please take anything you like from the dessert tray

디저트 아무거나 다 갖다 드세요

196
Would you like some?
좀 드실래요?

197
Would you like another drink?
한 잔 더 할래요?

198
Do you want some more?
더 들래요?

199
Have some more
좀 더 드세요

200
Do you want a bite of this?
이거 좀 더 들어볼래요?

201
I've had enough
많이 먹었어요

202
I'm (getting) full
배가 불러요

203
I'm stuffed
배불러

204

I'm on a diet

다이어트 중이야

NOTE

cuisine 조리법 recipe 조리법 baked (불에 대지 않고 열로) 구운 boiled 삶은, 끓인 broiled 구운 casserole 냄비요리 fried 튀긴 grilled (가스나 숯불 위에서) 구운 marinated 절인 raw 날 것의 roasted 불로 구운 sauteed 뜨거운 불판에 빨리 익힌 skewered 꼬치 smoked 훈제 stuffed 속을 넣은 steamed 찐 stewed 졸인 well-done 잘 익힌 rare 덜 익힌 medium-rare 알맞게 덜 익힌 medium 알맞게 익힌

9 음식 맛있냐고 물어보기

205

How do you like the steak?

고기 맛이 어때?

206

How do you like the food?

음식이 어때?

207

How was the meal?

식사 어땠어요?

208

How's the food?

맛이 어때?

209

Does your soup taste all right?

수프 맛이 괜찮아?

210 ## Does it taste good?

맛이 좋아?

211 ## Is this delicious?

맛있어?

212 ## This looks great[good; delicious]

이거 맛있게 보인다

213 ## This smells great

냄새가 좋은데

214 ## This is so good

맛 좋다

215 ## It's good

맛 좋아

216 ## It's delicious

맛있어

217 ## That was good

맛 좋았어

218 It was delicious

맛있었어

219 This is the best steak I've eaten in a long time

이렇게 맛난 스테이크는 오랜만에 처음야

220 It doesn't taste good

맛이 안 좋아

221 This doesn't taste as good as it looks

보기처럼 맛있지 않아

222 This has a strong flavor

맛이 너무 강해

223 It's spicy[sweet]

매워[달아]

224 It's (too) salty

(너무) 짜

225 It's too greasy

기름기가 너무 많아

226 ## It's too hot

너무 뜨거워

227 ## This sauce is so spicy. It's making my mouth burn

소스가 매워. 입이 탄다 타

228 ## My mouth is burning[on fire]

입이 타

229 ## This tastes strange[weird]

이건 맛이 넘 이상해

230 ## This yogurt tastes odd

이 요구르트는 맛이 이상해

231 ## This ham must be past its due date

이 햄은 유효기간이 지났을거야

232 ## I hope you enjoyed your meal

식사 맛있었길 바래

233 ## We enjoyed it very much

아주 맛있게 먹었어

234 You're a good cook

너 참 요리 잘 한다

235 I'm afraid this steak is over done

고기가 너무 구워진 것 같아

10 술과 담배에 관해 표현들

236 Here's to you!

당신을 위해 건배!, 너한테 주는 선물이야!

237 Here's to your health!

당신의 건강을 위하여!

238 I'd like to propose a toast

축배를 듭시다

239 Let me propose a toast to Mr. Kim

미스터 김을 위해 건배할게요

240 Let's drink to Miss Park's future!

미스 박의 미래를 위해서 건배합시다!

241 Bottoms up!

위하여!

242 Cheers!

건배!

243 Say when

됐으면 말해

244 How about a drink?

술 한잔 어때

245 I need a drink

술 한잔 해야겠어

246 Would you like to have a drink after work?

퇴근 후 한잔 할테야?

247 How much do you usually drink?

보통 술 얼마나 마셔?

248 He's a heavy drinker

갠 술 잘 마셔

249 I can drink a lot

술 많이 마실 수 있어

250 I have a hangover

술이 아직 안 깼나봐

251 I'm suffering from a hangover today

오늘 아직 숙취가 있어

252 I get drunk easily

난 쉽게 취해

253 I feel a little tipsy

아직 취기가 있어

254 I'm loaded[drunk]

술 취했어

255 Please don't drink too much

너무 과음하지마

256 I don't drink

난 술 안마셔

257 # I prefer draft beer
생맥주가 좋아

258 # I don't smoke anymore
더 이상 담배 안펴

259 # I quit smoking
담배 끊었어

260 # I stopped smoking
이제 담배 안펴

261 # How many packs a day?
하루에 몇 갑이나 펴?

262 # I'm a chain[heavy] smoker
난 줄담배 펴

263 # Can I bum a smoke?
담배 한가치 줄래?

264 # Do you serve alcohol?
알코올 팔아요?

265 What kind of beer would you like?

어떤 맥주를 드릴까요?

266 What do you have?

뭐가 있어요?

267 We have Budweiser and Heineken

버드와이저하고 하이네켄이 있어요

268 I'll have a Bud

버드로 주세요

269 Give me a cocktail, not so strong, please

세지 않은 칵테일 주세요

270 Let me buy you a drink

술 한잔 살게

11 식당에서 포장하기

271
Is that for here or to go?
여기서 드실 겁니까, 가지고 가실 겁니까?

272
Will this be for here or to go?
여기서 드실거예요 아니면 포장예요?

273
For here or to go?
여기서요 아니면 포장요?

274
For here, please
여기서 먹을게요

275
Can I get it to go?
포장되나요?

276
I'd like it to go, please
포장으로 해줘요

277
(Do you want to) Eat here or take it out?
여기서 드실래요 아니면 포장인가요?

Chapter 05

278 **Will that be to go?**

가져가실 건가요?

279 **Take-out?**

포장요?

280 **Can we get take-out?**

포장돼요?

281 **Will you make it for takeout?**

포장해주실래요?

282 **Could I[we] have a doggie bag, please?**

포장지 좀 줄래요?

283 **Could you pack the rest of the meal for take-out?**

남은 음식 가져가게 싸줄래요?

284 **I'd like to take it with me. Can you pack it up, please?**

가져갈게요. 포장해줄래요?

03 결재

12 식당에서 지불하기

285
It's on me
내가 낼게

286
This one is on me
이번엔 내가 낼게

287
It's on the house
이건 서비스입니다

288
I'll pick up the tab[check]
내가 계산할게

289
Let me pick up the tab
내가 계산할게

290
Let me take care of the bill
내가 계산할게

291
This is my treat
내가 살게

292 I'll treat you

내가 대접하죠

293 This is my round

이건 내가 쏜다

294 It's my treat this time

이번은 내가 대접하는거야

295 I'm buying

내가 살게

296 I'll pay for dinner

저녁은 내가 낼게

297 Where is the cashier?

계산대가 어디죠?

298 Does the price of this course include drink?

이 코스가격에 술도 포함된 건가요?

299 (I'd like the) Check, please

계산서 좀 주세요

300 I'd like to pay the bill, please

계산을 좀 하려구요

301 Could you bring me my bill?

계산서 갖다 줄래요?

302 What's the damage?

얼마죠?

303 What is this charge for?

이거 얼마입니까?

304 How much is the total?

총 얼마입니까?

305 I'll pay. What's the total?

내가 낼게요. 전부 얼마예요?

306 May I have a receipt, please?

영수증 주실래요?

307 Is tax included?

세금이 포함된 건가요?

308 Here is a little something for you

이건 얼마 안되지만 팁이에요

309 Please include the tip with my credit card

카드결재할 때 팁도 넣어요

310 How much should I leave on the table?

테이블에 얼마 남겨야 돼?

311 What kind of tip should I leave?

팁 몇 프로를 남겨둬야 돼?

312 We'd like[We want] to pay separately

각자 내려고요

313 Let's go halves

반반 내자

314 Let me share the bill

나도 반 낼게

315 Let's split the bill

나누어 내자

316 Let's go Dutch

자기가 먹은 건 자기가 내자

317 How much is my share?

내 몫은 얼마지?

318 How much is mine?

난 얼마야?

319 Can I pay with my credit card?

카드로 내도 돼요?

320 Can I use a credit card?

카드 돼요?

321 What kind of card can we use?

무슨 카드 돼요?

322 I'd like to pay in cash

현금으로 낼게요

323 Is the service charge included?

팁도 포함된 가격인가요?

324 I think the calculation is wrong

계산이 잘못 된 것 같아요

325 There's a mistake in the bill

계산서에 틀린 곳이 있네요

Chapter

06

건강 운동

01 상담

1 건강에 관한 일반적인 표현들

001
How do you feel?
오늘 기분 어때?

002
Are you (feeling) okay?
기분 괜찮아?

003
You don't look very well
오늘 안 좋아 보여

004
You look pale
창백해 보여

005
You look like you've lost weight lately
최근 너 살 빠진 것 같아

006
Are you all right?
괜찮아?

007
Are you well again?
다시 괜찮아졌어?

008 Are you back to normal?

다시 좋아 진거야?

009 Are you in good shape?

건강 좋아?

010 I'm in good shape[health]

건강이 좋아

011 My biggest problem is my pot belly

불쑥 나온 배가 나의 가장 큰 문제야

012 What's your secret for staying healthy?

건강을 유지하는 비결이 뭐야?

013 Have you completely recovered?

완전히 회복된거야?

014 I feel better

기분이 나아졌어

015 I don't feel any better

하나도 나아진 게 없어

016 **I always stop eating before I feel full**

난 항상 배가 부르기까지 먹지 않아

017 **I keep early hours**

일찍 일어나

018 **I always get enough sleep**

충분히 수면을 취해

019 **You should quit smoking**

넌 담배 끊는게 나아

020 **I gave up smoking for my health**

건강 때문에 담배 끊었어

021 **Do you get regular physical check-ups?**

정기적으로 건강검진을 받아?

022 **I get a dental check-up every six months**

6개월마다 치과에서 정기검진 받아

023 **I get a cancer check-up once a year**

일년에 한번 암검사를 받아

024 Have you had your hepatitis shot yet?

아직 간염주사 안 맞았니?

025 Nothing can take the place of good health

건강만큼 중요한 게 없어

hospital 종합병원 clinic 진료소 community hospital 지역병원 hospice 안락원 mental hospital 정신병원 field hospital 야전병원 emergency room 응급실 sickroom 병실 operating room 수술실 examination room 진찰실 delivery room 분만실 recovery room 회복실 outpatient 외래환자 inpatient 입원환자 case 환자 contract the disease 병에 걸리다 be hospitalized (be in the hospital) 입원하다 stethoscope 청진기 thermometer 체온계 blood pressure machine 혈압계 first visit 초진 revisit 재진 diagnosis 진단 check-up 건강진단 medical certificate 진단서 medical history 병력 family history 가족병 injection 주사 treatment 치료 transfusion 수혈 trauma 외상 doctor's round 회진 house call 왕진 hygiene 위생 oral medicine 내복약 application 외용약 tablet; pill 정제

Chapter 06

2 병원에 가서 진찰받기

026 I'd like to see the doctor

진찰 좀 받고 싶은데요

027 You'd better go see a doctor

병원에 가봐야 돼

028 Please call a doctor

의사 좀 불러요

029 Could you send me a doctor?

의사 좀 보내줄래요?

030 Please take me to the hospital

병원으로 데려다 주세요

031 Please take me to the nearest hospital

가장 가까운 병원으로 데려다주세요

032 Can you find a doctor who speaks Korean?

한국말 하는 의사 좀 찾아주실래요?

033 Do you need a doctor?

의사가 필요하세요?

034 Can I buy medicine without prescription?

처방전없이 약 살 수 있어요?

035 Please call an ambulance

앰블런스 불러줘요

036 I want to know what's wrong with me

어디가 안 좋은지 알고 싶어요

037 I've come for a consultation about general health

전반적인 건강상태를 상담하러 왔어요

038 How is my overall health, doctor?

전반적인 건강상태가 어떤가요, 선생님?

039 I want to have my blood examined

혈압 좀 재주세요

040 Your blood pressure is stable now

혈압은 이제 정상입니다

041 I've never had any trouble with my health

건강엔 전혀 문제가 없었어요

042 Give me medicine for a cold, please

감기약 주세요

043 What's wrong?

어디가 아파요?

044 What's wrong with you?

어디가 아프세요?

045 **What's your complaint?**

어디가 아프세요?

046 **What's the matter[trouble]?**

어디가 아프세요?

047 **Is (there) anything wrong?**

어디 안 좋은데 있어요?

048 **Where does it hurt?**

어디가 아파요?

049 **Where is the pain?/**
Where do you have pain?

어디가 아프세요?

050 **Where do you feel the pain most?**

어느 부위가 가장 아파요?

051 **What are your symptoms?/**
What symptoms do you have?

증상이 어때요?

052
Let me check your temperature
체온 좀 재볼게요

053
Let me check your blood pressure
혈압 좀 재볼게요

054
Is there a history of heart disease in your family?
가족 중 심장병 앓은 분이 있나요?

055
How's your vision?
시력이 어떠세요?

056
Did you eat something unusual?
좀 색다른 거 드셨나요?

057
Do you still feel pain?
통증이 느껴지나요?

058
What kind of pain is it?
어떤 종류의 통증인가요?

059
Do you have pain anywhere else?
다른 데 아픈 곳이 있나요?

060 Do you have a high temperature?

열이 많이 나요?

061 Do you have a fever?

열이 있어요?

062 Do you have a cold?

감기 걸렸어요?

063 Do you have a severe headache?

두통이 심한가요?

064 Do you have a sore throat?

인후염이 있나요?

065 Do you feel nauseous?

속이 울렁거리나요?

066 Do you have a diarrhea?

설사하세요?

067 Are you allergic to any kind of medication?

특정 약에 알러지 있나요?

068 Does anyone in your family suffer from diabetes?

가족 중에 당뇨병 환자 있나요?

069 Do you suffer from insomnia?

불면증에 시달리나요?

070 Do you suffer from back pain?

등 통증에 시달립니까?

071 When was your last bowel movement?

마지막으로 변을 본 것이 언제지요?

072 How long have you had a problem with indigestion?

소화불량으로 얼마나 고생했나요?

073 Have you ever fractured your leg before?

전에 다리가 부러진 적 있습니까?

074 That's a nasty bruise. How did it happen?

타박상이 심하군요. 어쩌다 그랬어요?

075 Are you taking any medication?

치료는 받고 있나요?

076 Are you taking any medicine regularly?

정기적으로 먹는 약 있어요?

077 I'm not taking any medicine

먹는 약 없어요

078 Have you had your wisdom teeth pulled out?

사랑니 뽑았어요?

079 How long have you had this pain?

이 통증이 시작한 지 얼마나 되었나요?

080 Since when has it hurt?

언제부터 아픈가요?

081 When did it start?

언제부터 그래요?

082 When did this trouble start?

이 통증이 언제 시작되었나요?

083 How long has it been bothering you?

얼마동안 고생하신거예요?

084 How is your appetite?

식욕은 어때요?

085 Does it (still) hurt?

(아직) 아픈가요?

086 Does it hurt much?

많이 아파요?

087 Does it hurt all the time?

계속 아파요?

088 Does it hurt when I touch it?

만지면 아픈가요?

089 Do I have to come to the hospital every day?

매일 병원에 와야 하나요?

090 Should I be hospitalized?

입원해야 하나요?

091 How long will you be in the hospital for?

얼마나 입원해 있어야 하는거야?

092 Will I be able to get well soon?

곧 좋아질까요?

093 How long does it take to get over this?

낫는데 시간이 얼마나 걸릴까요?

094 Do I need an operation?/ Will surgery be necessary?

수술해야 하나요?

095 Will surgery cure it?

수술하면 나을까요?

096 Is it all right to drink?

술을 마셔도 됩니까?

097 What foods should I avoid?

어떤 음식을 피해야 하나요?

098 What about my diet?

내 식이요법은 어떻게 하나요?

099 You'd better eat something that's easy to digest

소화가 잘 되는 것으로 드세요

100 I had shrimp last night

지난 밤에 새우를 먹었어요

101 Maybe the raw food for lunch was bad

아마도 점심으로 먹은 날 음식이 상했던 것 같아요

3 감기 등 몸이 안 좋아

102
I'm not feeling very well
몸이 아주 안 좋아요

103
I don't feel well
몸이 좋지 않아요

104
It hurts here
여기가 아파요

105
I have a pain here
여기가 통증이 있어요

106
I get tired easily
쉽게 피곤해져요

107
I'm getting fat
살이 쪄

108
I've put on[gained] weight
살 쪘어

109 **I tend to put on weight easily**

난 살이 쉽게 찌는 스타일야

110 **I feel sluggish**

피곤해

111 **I caught a cold**

감기 걸렸어

112 **I have a bad cold**

감기가 심해

113 **I've got the flu**

유행성 감기에 걸렸어

114 **I caught a cold from you**

감기 너한테 옮았나봐

115 **There's a bad cold going around**

독감이 유행야

116 **I have a runny nose**

코가 흘러

117 My nose is running

코가 흘러

118 My nose won't stop running

코가 멈추지 않고 계속 흘러

119 I can't stop coughing

기침이 멈추지 않아요

120 I feel chilly

으실으실 추워

121 I don't have any appetite

식욕이 없어

122 I have only a small appetite

식욕이 별로 없어

NOTE

specialist 전문의　resident 레지던트　intern 인턴　family doctor 주치의　midwife 산파
veterinarian 수의사　therapist 심리치료사　pharmacist 약제사　surgery 외과　surgeon
외과의　internal medicine 내과　physician 내과의　neurology 신경과　neurologist 신
경과의　psychiatry 정신과　psychiatrist 정신과의　eye doctor 안과의　dentistry 치과
dentist 치과의　urology 비뇨기과　urologist 비뇨기과의

4 머리, 코, 입, 눈 그리고 귀가 아파

123
I have a slight[terrible] headache
머리가 조금 (아주) 아파

124
I always suffer from this headache
항상 이 두통으로 고생하고 있어

125
This part of my head particularly aches
머리의 이쪽 부분이 아파

126
My head hurts
머리가 아파

127
My head feels heavy
머리가 무거워

Chapter 06

128
I have a migraine
편두통이 있어

129
I get a headache when I wear my glasses
안경을 쓰면 머리가 아파

130 I suffer from halitosis

난 입냄새가 나요

131 I'm afraid I have bad breath

내가 입냄새가 나는 것 같아요

132 It aches when I open my mouth

입을 벌릴 때 아파요

133 I have a swollen tongue

혀가 부었어요

134 My lips are[My mouth is] dry and rough

입[술]이 마르고 거칠어요

135 I have a toothache

치통이 있어

136 My tooth hurts

이가 아파

137 My tooth is killing me

이 아파 죽겠어

138

One of my teeth in the back hurts

어금니 중 하나가 아파요

139

I have two decayed teeth

충치가 2개 있어요

140

I have a cavity in one of my lower back teeth and it hurts

아래 어금니중 하나가 충치인데 아파요

141

It hurts so much I can't sleep at night

너무 아파서 밤에 잠을 못자요

142

When I chew on something, a sharp pain shoots through my jaw

뭔가 씹을 때 심한 통증이 턱을 관통해요

143

Even a slight touch to the tooth is intensely painful

이를 약간 대기만 해도 엄청 아파요

144

The tooth smarts when I eat something cold

뭔가 차가운 걸 먹을 때 이가 쑤셔요

145 When I drink something cold, there is a sharp pain

차가운 음료를 마실 때 통증이 심해요

146 The tooth hurts when food touches it

이가 음식에 닿으면 아파요

147 I can't chew my food well because of a toothache

치통 때문에 음식을 잘 못 씹어요

148 I have a loose tooth

이가 흔들려요

149 My teeth feel loose and I have difficulty in chewing

이가 흔들리는 것 같아 씹기 어려워요

150 The gums ache if I press them with my finger

손가락으로 누르면 잇몸이 아파요

151 The wisdom tooth aches

사랑니가 아파요

152

I want to have this tooth pulled out

이 이를 빼주세요

153

I want to have this cavity filled

이 충치를 치료해주세요

154

I want to have a false tooth put in

틀니를 넣어주세요

155

I have a sore throat/ My throat's sore

목이 아파요

156

I've got a really sore throat

목이 정말 아파요

157

My throat feels raw

목소리가 쑤셔요

158

I have an irritated throat

목에 염증이 있어요

159

My throat hurts when I swallow

삼킬 때 목이 아파요

160 My throat is swollen

목이 부었어요

161 I think my tonsils are swollen

편도선이 부었어요

162 I'm a little nearsighted

약간 근시(近視)예요

163 My eyes are sore

눈이 아파요

164 When I close my eyes, they hurt

눈을 감을 때 아파요

165 My eyes feel hot[itchy, tired]

눈이 충혈돼요[간지러워요, 피로해요]

166 My eyes feel irritated

눈에 염증이 있어요

167 When I look at close things, my eyes get tired

가까운 것을 볼 때 눈이 피로해져요

168 # My vision is blurred

시력이 침침해졌어요

169 # I'm afraid I have an ear infection

귀에 염증이 있어요

170 # I have a ringing in my ears

귀가 멍멍해요

171 # My ear hurts terribly when I touch it

귀를 만지면 엄청 아파요

172 # At first it didn't hurt so much, but now there is a throbbing pain

처음에는 별로 안 아팠는데 지금은 욱신거려요

173 # The pain increases at night. It throbs so much I can't get to sleep

밤에 통증이 심해져요. 욱신거려서 잠잘 수가 없어요

174 # I'm a little hard of hearing these days

요즘 좀 난청이예요

175 It's difficult to catch what people say

사람들이 말하는 걸 알아 듣지 못하겠어요

176 I have a cold and sneeze a lot

감기가 걸려서 재채기가 심해요

177 Once I start sneezing, I can't stop

재채기를 하기 시작하면 멈출 수가 없어요

178 I have a running nose

콧물이 나요

179 My nose is running terribly and I have a headache

콧물이 심하게 나서 머리가 아파요

180 When I blow my nose, my ears squeak

코를 풀 때 귀가 삐꺽거려요

181 I have a nose bleed every morning

매일 아침 코피가 흘러요

182 My nose often bleeds

코에서 가끔 피가 나요

5 혈관, 심장, 배 등이 아플 때

183

I have high[low] blood pressure

고[저]혈압야

184

I[My head] feel dizzy

어지러워

185

There is a sudden sharp pain in my chest

갑작스럽게 심한 가슴통증이 났어요

186

Doctor, my chest is killing me

의사 선생님, 가슴이 너무 아파요

187

I have a heavy feeling in my chest

가슴이 무겁게 느껴져요

188

I feel as if it is hard to breath

숨쉬기가 힘들게 느껴져요

189

I have heart disease

심장병이 있어요

190

I feel as if I have a convulsion in my heart

심장발작이 있는 것 같아요

191 I suffer from asthma
천식이예요

192 My fever has gone down
열이 내려갔어

193 I'm running a fever
열이 나

194 I think I have a fever
열이 있는 것 같아

195 I have a bit of a fever
열이 좀 있어

196 I have a high temperature
열이 높아

197 I have a stomachache
복통야

198 I'm troubled with chronic stomachaches
만성복통으로 아파

199 My stomach's upset
배탈났어

200 I have food poisoning
식중독야

201 I've got the runs
설사했어요

202 I have diarrhea
설사했어요

203 I have dull pain in the stomach
배가 뻐근해요

204 I have a squeezing pain in the stomach
배가 쥐어짜듯이 아파요

205 Sometimes, there is a sharp pain at the upper right-hand side of my stomach
때때로 오른 쪽 윗배 심한 통증이 있어요

206 It hurts all around my stomach. Especially when I cough and breathe deeply

배 주변 전체가 아파요. 특히 재채기를 하거나 숨을 깊게 쉴 때 아파요

207 Whenever my stomach is empty, it begins to hurt

공복시마다 아프기 시작해요

208 My stomach aches after meals

식후에 배가 아파요

209 I don't feel well in my stomach

배가 좋지 않아요

210 I always feel uncomfortable in my stomach

배가 항상 좋지 않아요

211 My stomach hurts and I feel like vomiting

배가 아프고 토할 것 같아요

212 I have a pain in the upper abdomen when I'm hungry

배가 고프면 윗배가 아파요

213 I have a pain in my side

옆구리가 아파요

214 I have a pain in the lower abdomen

아랫배가 아파요

215 I feel pain from indigestion

소화불량예요

216 My stomach feels bloated and I have no appetite

복부가 팽창되어 있고 식욕이 없어요

Chapter 06

217 I have gas in the stomach

복부에 가스가 찼어요

218 I always have the feeling of hunger

항상 배가 고파요

219 I have upset stomach

복통이예요

220 I have indigestion

소화불량예요

221 I feel like throwing up

토할 것 같아

222 I feel nauseated

토할 것 같아

223 I feel like vomiting and I have the hiccups

토할 것 같고 딸꾹질이 나요

NOTE

long-sightedness 원시 short-sightedness(근시) bronchitis 기관지염 insomnia 불면증 Alzheimer's disease 치매 amnesia 건망증 suffer from hallucinations 환각 phobia 공포증 megalomania 과대 망상증 faint 실신하다 character disorder 성격이상 paralysis 마비 sleepwalking 몽유병 throw a fit 발작하다 vomiting 구토 chill 오한 ulcer 궤양 hepatitis 간염 diarrhea[runs] 설사 suffer from constipation 변비로 고생하다 bowel movement 배변 food poisoning 식중독 gastritis 위염 indigestion 소화불량 heart disease 심장병 heart attack 심장마비 heart failure 심부전 obesity 비만 hemorrhoids 치질 cast 깁스붕대 prostate cancer 전립선 암

6 쥐, 마비, 골절 등

224 I've got a really stiff neck

목이 너무 뻣뻣해서요

225 My neck is so stiff that I can't move

목이 너무 뻣뻣해서 움직이지 못하겠어요

226

My neck is so painful that I can't turn it

목이 너무 아파서 돌릴 수가 없어요

227

I strained my neck and can't move my head

목이 삐어서 머리를 움직이지 못하겠어요

228

I have a sharp pain if I try to turn my head

머리를 돌릴려고 하면 통증이 심해요

229

My neck snapped when I suddenly put on the brakes

급작스럽게 브레이크를 밟았을 때 머리가 젖혀졌어요.

230

Lately when I get up, my shoulders hurt very much

최근 일어날 때 어깨가 무척 아파요

231

I have stiff shoulders/ My shoulders are stiff

어깨가 뻣뻣해요

232

I've got a pain in my side

옆구리에 통증이 있어

233 I have a pain in my groin when I walk

걸을 때 사타구니 쪽이 아파요

234 I have severe pain in my back

등에 심한 통증이 있어요

235 My back hurts sometimes

등이 때때로 무척 아파요

236 My back itches

등이 간지러워요

237 I have a rash on my back

등에 뾰루지가 났어요

238 I suffer from back pain

요통이 있어요

239 When I was swinging my golf club, I suddenly felt a terrible pain and I haven't been able to move since

골프를 칠 때 갑작스러운 통증을 느꼈고 그 이후로는 움직이질 못하겠어요

240 When I try to straighten my back, the pain hits me

등을 펴려고 하면 통증이 와요

241 My legs have been cramping up

다리에 쥐가 났어요

242 I have a cramp in my thigh

허벅지에 쥐가 났어

243 I have cramps

쥐가 났어요

244 I sprained my ankle[finger]

발목(손)이 삐었어요

245 When I missed my step, I seem to have sprained my ankle

발을 헛디뎠을 때 발을 삔 것 같아요

246 I twisted my ankle

발목이 겹질러졌어요

247
I twisted my foot, and I'd like you to see if it's all right

발이 꼬였는데 괜찮은지 알고 싶어요

248
I broke my leg[arm]

다리가[손이] 부러졌어

249
I fell down the steps and seem to have broken my leg

계단에서 넘어져서 다리가 부러진 것 같아요

250
My arm hurts so much I can't reach my back

팔이 아파서 뒤로 뻗을 수가 없어요

251
My joints ache

관절이 아파요

252
I sometimes have a pain in my knees

무릎이 때때로 아파요

253
I have a swollen foot

발이 부었어요

254

My legs are swollen

다리가 부었어요

256

I fractured my left leg while skiing

스키타다 왼쪽 다리에 골절상을 입었어요

7 **기타 통증이나 병**

257

I'm a diabetic

당뇨예요

258

It's itchy

가려워요

259

It's bleeding

피가 나요

260

It hurts

아파요

261

Ouch!

애!

261

Is somebody hurt?

누가 다쳤어요?

262

My hiccups won't stop

딸꾹질이 멈추질 않아요

263

I burned my hand

손이 데였어

264

I have blisters on my palm

손바닥에 물집이 있어요

265

I got a sunburn on the beach

해변에서 햇볕에 탔어요

266

I've got a cut here

여기 칼로 베었어요

267

I cut my hand with a knife

칼로 손을 베었어요

268

When I urinate, it hurts terribly

소변을 눌 때 무척 아파요

269 It's difficult to urinate

소변누기가 힘들어요

270 I have severe frostbite on my hands

두 손에 심한 동상을 입었어요

271 My tennis elbow began to ache again

팔꿈치 통증이 다시 시작했어요

272 My limbs feel numb and paralyzed

사지가 무감각하고 마비됐어요

273 The wound is swollen

상처가 부었어요

274 The wound is inflamed

상처가 염증을 일으켰어요

275 I have red specks on my face

얼굴에 붉은 반점이 있어요

276 I have rashes all over my body

온 몸에 뽀루지가 났어요

277

I have severe hives

심한 두드러기가 났어요

278

I'm allergic to fish

생선에 앨러지가 있어요

279

The itching is quite unbearable

가려움 증이 정말 못 참을 정도예요

280

I feel itchy all over my body

온 몸이 가려워요

281

I think I'm about to have a nervous breakdown

신경 쇠약에 걸릴 것 같아

Chapter

07

쇼핑 · 구매

상황별 영어
대표문장

Common
Sentences
in Situation
English

이 구매

1 쇼핑할 곳 찾기

001

Tell me the closest shopping mall from here

여기서 가장 가까운 쇼핑몰을 알려주세요

002

Which floor has clothing items?

몇층에 의류가 있나요?

003

Where can I get some shoes?

신발을 어디에서 살 수 있어요?

004

Which floor has foods?

음식은 몇층에 있어요?

005

I'm looking for a discount shop

할인점을 찾고 있어요

006

Can you recommend any shops for buying gifts?

선물을 살 상점을 추천해줄래요?

007

Where is the stationery section?

문구 쪽은 어디인가요?

008
Are there any flea markets?

벼룩시장이 있나요?

009
Could you please draw a map?

약도 좀 그려줄래요?

010
Is this the accessory floor?

여기가 액세서리 파는 층인가요?

011
Where's a duty free shop?

면세점은 어디 있나요?

012
Can I buy things duty free here?

여기서 면세로 살 수 있나요?

013
Can I buy it tax-free?

면세로 살 수 있나요?

2 살 물건을 찾거나 그냥 구경하기

014
How may I help you?

어떻게 도와드릴까요?

015 How can I help[serve] you?

어떻게 도와드릴까요?

016 What can I do for you?

뭘 도와드릴까요?

017 Are you looking for anything special?

뭐 특별한 거 찾으시는거 있나요?

018 I'm looking for a gift for my mother

어머니 드릴 선물 찾고 있어요

019 (No thanks,) I'm already being helped

이미 다른 분이 봐주고 계세요

020 I'm just looking (around)

그냥 구경하고 있는거예요

021 (I'm) Just browsing

그냥 구경하는거예요

022 When do you open?

언제 열어요?

023 When is closing time?

언제 닫아요?

024 Eighth, please

8층 부탁해요

025 The eighth floor, please

8층 부탁해요

026 Going down? Going up?

내려가세요? 올라가세요?

027 Where can I find ladies' wear?

여성복은 어디 있어요?

028 What're you looking for?

뭘 찾으세요?

029 Are you looking for anything in particular?

특별히 뭐 찾는게 있습니까?

030 I'm looking for a jazz CD

재즈 CD를 찾는데요

031 I'm looking for a bag

가방을 찾는데요

032 I'd like a suit

옷을 사려고요

033 I want to buy a snowboard

스노보드를 사려고요

034 Do you have a shirt with a plainer pattern?

더 평범한 무늬의 셔츠 있어요?

035 Do you carry watch batteries?

시계 배터리 파세요?

036 I'm sorry, we don't carry that brand

미안해요, 그 브랜드는 취급 안해요

037 We're having a big sale this week

이번 주에 세일을 크게 해요

038 This is a hot sale item nowadays

요즘 잘 나가는 품목이예요

039 Are there any nice gifts for kids?

아이들 줄 멋진 선물 뭐 있나요?

040 I'm looking for a gift for my kid

아이들 선물 찾고 있어요

NOTE

department store 백화점 souvenir shop 기념품점 fitting room 탈의실 pure gold 순
금 tax-free items 면세품 return 반품하다 refund 환불하다 shopping center 쇼핑센터
convenience store 편의점 stationery shop 문구점 antique shop 골동품점 barber
shop 이발소 boutique (여성용 고급 유행복이나 액세서리를 파는) 가게, 상점

3 살 물건 결정하기

041 May I try it on?

입어봐도 돼요?

042 May I wear this?

입어봐도 되나요?

043 I'd like to try this on

이거 입어보고 싶어요

044 What kind of style is now in fashion?

지금 유행중인 스타일은 뭔가요?

Chapter 07

045 I'm looking for skirts which cost around 70 dollars

한 70달러 정도되는 치마를 찾고 있어요

046 Would you like to try it on?

입어보실래요?

047 Please show me this

이것 좀 보여주세요

048 Show me that ring, please

저 반지 좀 보여주세요

049 Show me another one, please

다른 것도 좀 보여주세요

050 Would you show me that one?

저것 좀 보여주실래요?

051 Do you have anything on sale?

세일 상품 뭐 있어요?

052 What brand do you prefer?

어느 브랜드를 좋아하세요?

053
Where is the fitting[dressing] room?
탈의실이 어디예요?

054
It's too small[big] for me
내게 너무 작[크]네요

055
It's a little bit tight
너무 쪼이네요

056
Could you please show me another jacket?
다른 쟈켓 보여줄래요?

057
Do you have them in any other colors?
이거 다른 색상으로 있나요?

058
What is your size?
사이즈가 어떻게 돼요?

Chapter 07

059
I don't know sizes in this country
여기 사이즈는 잘 모르겠는데요

060
Would you measure me?
제 치수 좀 재 주시겠어요?

061

Do you have this in my size?

이거 제 사이즈 있나요?

062

What size do you wear?

사이즈가 어떻게 돼요?

063

Would you have one in a smaller size?

좀 더 작은 사이즈 있어요?

064

Do you have this shirt in a smaller size?

이 셔츠 작은 사이즈 있어요?

065

This is too loose. Do you have a smaller one?

너무 헐렁해요. 더 작은거 있어요?

066

It's too tight[loose, short, long] for me

내게 너무 쪼여요[헐렁해요, 짧아요, 길어요]

067

Do you have a bigger size?

더 큰 사이즈 있나요?

068

Can you make it in my size?

제 사이즈로 맞출 수 있어요?

069

Is there any other sizes?

다른 사이즈 있어요?

070

Do you have another type in this color?

이 색깔로 다른 타입 있나요?

071

Do you have this in black?

이거 검은 색 있나요?

072

Do you have any other designs?

다른 디자인 있어요?

073

How's this?

이건 어때요?

074

Does it look good on me?

내게 잘 어울려요?

Chapter **07**

075

The skirt matches this blouse, doesn't it?

이 치마가 이 블라우스랑 어울리죠 그렇죠?

076

This skirt and this blouse go together well

이 치마와 이 블라우스가 잘 어울려요

077 Can you help me choose a dress?

드레스를 고르는거 도와드릴까요?

078 Do you have different colors?

다른 색 있어요?

079 Please show me the jacket in the display window

진열장에 있는 자켓 좀 보여주세요

080 Can I try some other clothes?

다른 옷들 입어볼 수 있나요?

081 Where is the fitting room?

탈의실이 어디인가요?

082 Could you alter this?

이거 수선돼요?

083 Are alterations free?

수선비는 공짜예요?

084 Can this be machine washed?

세탁기로 세탁해도 돼요?

085 Is this laundry washable?

세탁기로 세탁 가능해요?

086 What age is this good for?

어떤 나이에 어울리나요?

087 Which perfume is popular?

어떤 향수가 유행하나요?

088 Give me five of the same thing

같은 걸로 5개 주세요

089 Do you have the same as this?

이거랑 같은 거 있어요?

090 May I touch this?

이거 만져봐도 돼요?

091 What brand is this?

이거는 어디 브랜드인가요?

092 Where is this made?

이건 어디서 만들었나요?

093 Is this made in the USA?

이거 미국산인가요?

094 What is this made of?

이건 뭘로 만들었나요?

095 What material is this?

이거 재료는 무엇인가요?

096 Is this real leather?

이거 진짜 가죽예요?

097 Is this hand-made?

수공예 작품인가요?

098 I'll take three of them

저걸로 3개 주세요

099 Do you have better quality ones?

더 나은 제품이 있나요?

100 Thanks, but it's not what I want

감사하지만 제가 원하는 게 아니네요

101

This is nice

이거 좋은데요

102

This is better

이게 더 나아요

103

I like this better

이게 더 좋아요

104

I'll take[get] this one

이것으로 할게요

105

I'd like this one

이걸로 주세요

106

I'd like to buy this one

이거 살게요

107

It looks good on you

잘 어울리네요

108

Will that be all?

달리 더 필요한 것은 없으십니까?

109 Is that everything?

다 되셨습니까?

110 Will there be anything else?

더 필요한 건 없습니까?

결재

4 값 흥정하기

111

How much do I owe you?

내가 얼마를 내야 돼죠?, 얼마죠?

112

What do I owe you?

얼마인가요?

113

What's the damage?

얼마예요?

114

How much?

얼마예요?

115

How much is the total?

전부 얼마예요?

116

What is the total?

총액이 얼마인가요?

117

What's the price of this?

이거 가격이 어떻게 돼요?

118 How much does it cost?

이거 가격이 얼마예요?

119 How much is this?

이거 얼마예요?

120 What's that in dollars?

달러로는 얼마예요?

121 It's twenty dollars, including tax

세금포함해서 20달러예요

122 I have only 30 dollars now

지금 단 30달러만 갖고 있어요

123 How much can you afford to spend?

예산은 얼마쯤 잡고 계시는데요?

124 What's your budget?

예산은 얼마로 잡고 계신데요?

125 How much would you like to spend?

얼마정도 쓰실려구요?

126 **I'd like to get something for around 50 dollars**

50달러 정도로 사려구요

127 **I don't want to spend more than 30 dollars**

30달러 내에서 쓰고 싶어요

128 **I can't afford to buy it**

그걸 살 여유가 없어

129 **I can't afford it**

살 여유가 없어

130 **That's expensive!**

무척 비싸구만!

131 **How expensive!**

엄청 비싸네!

132 **That's too much!**

너무 비싸다!

133 **It's a bargain**

싸다, 싸잖아

134 **That's cheap!**

야 싸다!

135 **How cheap!**

정말 싸다!

136 **It's a real good buy at that price**

그 가격이면 진짜 잘 사는거야

137 **Wow, that's a steal!**

와, 거저네!

138 **At 40 percent below market, this is a good buy**

40% 할인가면 잘 산 거지요

139 **Can[Would] you give me a discount?**

좀 깎아 주실래요?

140 **If it was a little cheaper, I could buy it**

좀만 싸면 살 수 있을 텐데요

141 **If you discount I'll buy**

깎아주면 살게요

142

Can you give me a discount for paying cash?

현금내면 할인해줘요?

143

Can you make it cheaper?

좀 더 싸게 안돼요?

144

I'll take ten. So, would you give me a discount?

10개 살건데 깎아주실래요?

145

Can you make it a little cheaper?

좀 더 싸게 안돼요?

146

Sorry, we can't. This is our last price

죄송해요, 안돼요. 이게 마지막 가격입니다

147

That's over my budget. Could you give me a 20 dollars discount?

예산보다 비싸서 그런데 20달러 깎아줄래요?

148

Do you give discounts for cash?

현금이면 깎아주나요?

149

I'm sorry, I can't take a penny off

죄송하지만 한 푼도 못 깎아드려요

150 Take it or leave it

사시던지 아님 그냥 가세요

151 That's my final offer

내가 하는 마지막 제안예요

152 I got it at a bargain price

싼 가격에 그걸 샀어

153 Please show me less expensive one

좀 더 싼 걸로 보여주세요

154 Anything cheaper?

더 싼거는요?

155 My friend will also buy here

내 친구도 여기서 살거예요

156 This is 5 dollars at another store

다른 가게에서는 5달러예요

157 I picked it up at a flea market for $5

벼룩시장에서 5달러에 샀어

158   I bought this on impulse

이거 충동구매했어

159   I got it for next to nothing

거의 거저에 샀어

160   I bought this for almost nothing

거의 거저에 산거야

161   Can I make a down payment now and pay the rest later when I pick it up?

먼저 보증금내고 나중에 가져갈 때 나머지를 내도 되나요?

162   (Will that be) Cash or charge?

현금으로요 아니면 신용카드로요?

163   Would you like to pay by cash or charge?

현금으로 낼래요 아님 신용카드로 낼래요?

164   How would you like to pay for this?

어떻게 계산하실래요?

COMMON
SENTENCES
IN SITUATION
ENGLISH

5 산 물건의 값을 치를 때

165
Do you take checks?

수표 받나요?

166
Do you accept traveler's checks?

여행자수표 받아요?

167
Do you accept[take] Visa?

비자카드 받아요?

168
I'd like to pay for it by card. Do you take Visa?

카드로 결제할게요. 비자카드 되나요?

169
Can I use VISA?

비자카드 돼나요?

170
Can I pay in Korean won?

한국 원화로 낼 수 있어요?

171
Cash, please

현금으로요

172
I'll charge it, please

카드로 낼게요

173

I'll pay by check

수표로 낼게요

174

I'd like to buy it on credit

신용카드로 낼게요

175

I think there's something wrong with the amount

계산이 잘못된 것 같은데요

176

I'm afraid this isn't the correct change

잔돈이 안 맞는 것 같아요

177

I think your calculation is wrong

계산이 틀린 것 같아요

178

Can I have a receipt, please?

영수증을 받을 수 있을까요?

179

Here is your change and receipt

여기 잔돈과 영수증요

180

Is it OK to sign here?

여기에 사인하면 돼요?

181 Can I have these delivered to this address?

이 주소로 배달돼요?

182 Please deliver it to my home

이거 집으로 배달해줘요

183 Would you like these items delivered?

이 물건들을 배달해 드릴까요?

184 Do you send packages overseas?

해외로 배송하나요?

NOTE

I'd like to send this by air mail 항공우편으로 이걸 발송해주세요 Do you have weight limits? 무게 제한이 있습니까? I'd like to insure this package 이 짐에 보험을 들게요 I'd like to send this parcel to Korea 이 짐들을 한국으로 보내주세요 Where can I buy stamps? 우표를 어디서 사나요? How much is the postage? 우표값이 얼마인가요? Is there a post office near here? 근처에 우체국이 있나요? Is anything fragile in it? 안에 깨지는 물건이 뭐 있나요? Registered mail, please 등기우편으로요 zip code 우편번호 sender 발송

6 배송부탁하기

185
Please send it to this address by ship[air plane]

선편[항공편]으로 이 주소로 보내주세요

186
You can wrap these together

이것들 함께 포장해주세요

187
Could you please tie it with a ribbon?

리본 달아주실래요?

188
Can you put a ribbon on it?

리본 달아줄래요?

189
Please wrap it

포장해주세요

Chapter 07

190 Wrap as a gift, please

선물로 포장해주세요

7 반품 및 클레임

191 I still haven't received the merchandise I ordered

주문한거 아직 못 받았어요

192 I didn't receive the same merchandise I ordered

주문한거랑 다른게 왔어요

193 This is different from what I bought

구매한거랑 다른 제품이 왔어요

194 The merchandise I received was damaged

주문한 물품이 손상이 됐어요

195 Here is a crack

여기 금이 갔어요

196 I haven't used it at all

전혀 쓰지 않았어요

197 This size doesn't fit me

사이즈가 맞질 않아요

198 It doesn't fit me

나한테 안 맞아요

199 This is broken

부러졌어요

200 Have you dropped it?

떨어트렸나요?

201 It was broken from the beginning

처음부터 망가져있었어요

Chapter 07

202 Would you exchange it for me?

교환해줄래요?

203 I'd like to exchange this for something else

다른 걸로 교환해주세요

204 Please exchange it for a clean one

깨끗한 걸로 바꿔주세요

205 I'd like to return this

이거 반품할게요

206 Can I have[get] a refund?

환불되나요?

207 I'd like to get a refund, please

환불받고 싶어요

208 I'd like a refund, please

환불해 주세요

209 I'd like my money back, please

돈을 환불해주세요

210 I'd like to exchange this

이거 교환해주세요

211 Sorry, but exchange only, no refunds

죄송하지만 교환만 가능하고 환불은 안됩니다

Chapter

08

비즈니스

01 회사

1 직업, 직장, 그리고 출장에 관한 표현들

001 What do you do for a living?

직업이 뭐예요?

002 What do you do?

무슨 일 하세요?

003 Who do you work for?

어디서 일해?

004 I work for Mr. Anderson

앤더슨 씨 회사에서 일해

I work at[in]~ …에서 일해

005 I have been working here for 3 years

여기서 일한지 3년 됐어

006 He got fired

걘 해고됐어

007 I'm being transferred

나 전근 가

008

I hear you've been promoted

승진했다며

009

You changed jobs?

직업을 바꿨어?

010

I recently changed jobs

최근에 직업을 바꿨어

011

I'm between jobs

백수야

012

I'm thinking of retiring soon

퇴직할까 생각중야

013

I opted for early retirement last year

작년에 명예퇴직 신청했어

014

What are the (working) hours?

근무시간은?

015

Let's call it a day

퇴근합시다

016 Why don't we call it a day now?

오늘은 이제 그만 퇴근하자

017 Let's call it quits

퇴근합시다

018 Let's quit for today

오늘 그만 퇴근하죠

019 He's gone for the day

그 분은 퇴근했습니다

020 We're done for the day

그만 가자, 그만 하자

021 Are you working overtime tonight?

오늘밤 야근해?

022 I'm working nights

난 밤근무야

023 I have the night shift this week

이번주 밤근무야

024
I'll be out of town all next week

다음주 내내 출장갈거야

025
I'll be on the road most of next month

다음달 대부분 출장중일거야

026
Can you take care of my work while I'm away?

나 없을 때 내 일 좀 맡아줄래?

027
I have to call in sick

아파서 결근한다고 전화해야겠어

상황별 영어
대표문장

COMMON
SENTENCES
IN SITUATION
ENGLISH

02 업무

2 일을 지시할 때

028 **Please get it done by tomorrow morning**

내일 아침까지 마무리해

029 **Can you have the report done by 6 o'clock?**

6시까지 보고서 끝낼 수 있어?

030 **Finish this report today!**

오늘 이 보고서 끝내!

031 **Do this right away**

이거 지금 바로 해

032 **Please do this**

이거 해요

033 **Would you please do this for me?**

이것 좀 해줄래요?

034 **Do this when you can**

시간 될 때 해요

035 Please take care of this

이것 좀 처리하도록

036 Would you take a look at this paper?

이 서류 좀 한번 봐주실래요?

037 This is top priority

이게 최우선야

038 I want you to give this top priority

이거에 최우선을 두게

039 Please submit the document to me

이 문서를 내게 제출해요

040 Please hand the document in to me

이 문서를 내게 제출해요

041 This has to go out today

이건 오늘 나가야 돼

Chapter 08

042 Who is handling this account?

이 건은 누가 맡고 있어?

043 Who's going to handle the paperwork?

이 서류작업은 누가 맡을 건가?

044 That can't wait

이건 급해

045 This can wait

그건 나중에 해도 돼

046 Can't that wait?

미루면 안돼?, 급한거야?

047 You'd better work harder

더 열심히 일해라

048 Do your best!

최선을 다해!

049 Make sure they all know about it

걔들이 모두 알고 있도록 해

3 일을 시작할 때

050
Let's get down to business
자 일을 시작합시다

051
Let's get started
자 시작하자

052
Let's get started on the wedding plans
결혼식 계획을 실행하자

053
I gotta get started on my speech
연설을 시작하겠습니다

054
Let's roll
자 시작합시다

055
Let's get on with it
시작합시다

056
Get set[ready]!
준비해라!

057 Get ready for Christmas

크리스마스를 준비해

058 Get ready to run

뛸 준비해

0059 All right, are you ready?

좋아, 준비됐어?

060 Ready?

좋아, 준비됐어?

061 I'll go

내가 할게

062 All set

준비 다 됐어요

063 I'm[We're] all set

난[우린] 준비 다 됐어

064 We're ready

준비됐어요

065 I'll get to work on it right now

지금 바로 시작할게요

066 Just get to work

바로 일 시작해

067 I'll get right on it

당장 그렇게 하겠습니다

068 First things first

중요한 것부터 먼저 하자

069 Work comes first

일이 우선이야

070 I'm working on it

지금 하고 있어

071 I'm on it

내가 처리 중이야

072 I'll look it over first thing in the morning

내일 아침 일찍 바로 검토할게

COMMON
SENTENCES
IN SITUATION
ENGLISH

073   I'll do it immediately

당장 할게

---

④ **일의 진행상황을 알아보기**

074   When is this due?

마감일이 언제야?

075   When is the paper due?

이 서류 언제 마감야?

076   What's the due date?

마감일이 언제야?

077   It's due on the thirtieth

30일이 마감야

078   What's the deadline for this job?

이 일 마감이 언제야?

079   How much time do I have?

시간이 얼마나 있어?

080
The deadline is coming up

마감일이 다가오고 있어

081
The deadline's just a week away

마감일이 일주일 앞이야

082
We're behind schedule

일정보다 늦었어

083
The project is running a week behind schedule

그 프로젝트가 예정보다 일주일 늦고 있어

084
The schedule is just too demanding

일정이 너무 빡빡해

085
This is a tight schedule

일정이 빡빡하네

086
We're about two days ahead of schedule

일정보다 한 이틀 앞서가고 있어

087
When will it be ready?

언제 준비될까?

088 When does this have to be finished by?

이거 언제까지 끝내야 돼?

089 Is the report ready?

보고서 준비됐어?

090 Are the papers ready?

서류들 준비됐어?

091 Have you finished the report?

보고서 끝냈어?

092 What happened to the project?

그 프로젝트는 어떻게 됐어?

093 What happened to the documents I left here?

내가 여기 둔 문서는 어떻게 됐어?

094 We're still at it

아직도 하고 있어

095 There are no problems so far

지금까지는 아무 문제없어

096 Right now, things look pretty good
지금 상황은 꽤 좋아보여

097 It's moving right along
잘 되어 가고 있어

098 It's still in the planning stage
아직 기획단계예요

099 Nothing has been done about that project
그 프로젝트는 아직 된 게 없어

100 This paperwork is really a pain
이 서류작업은 정말 골칫거리야

101 We're finally getting somewhere
마침내 좀 진전했네요

102 We should start pushing them
걔들을 다그치기 시작해야겠어

103 That can't be done overnight
밤새 그렇게 한다는 건 불가능해요

5 최선을 다해 열심히 일하고 있다고 말하기

104 I did all I could do

난 할 수 있는 최선을 다 했어요

105 That's all I can do

이게 내가 할 수 있는 최선야

106 We're putting every effort into it

모든 노력을 기울이고 있어요

107 I have to work late today

오늘 야근해야 돼

108 I have to work overtime today

오늘 야근해야 돼

109 He's a hard worker

걘 일 열심히 하는 사람야

110 I'm a workaholic

난 일밖에 모르는 사람야

111 Let's see what happens

어떻게 되나 보자고

112 **I'll be sure to double-check everything from now on**

지금부터 철저히 확인할게요

113 **I'll try not to let you down**

실망하지 않도록 할게요

6 일을 끝냈는지 물어보기

114 **You done?**

다했어?

115 **Are you done with this?**

이거 끝냈니?

116 **Are you done with your meal?**

밥 다 먹었니?

117 **When will you be done with your work?**

언제까지면 일이 끝날 것 같아?

118 **I'm done with this**

이거 다 끝냈다

119 I'm (all) done with my work

이 일 (거의) 다 끝냈어

120 All done!

다 끝냈어!

121 It's done

끝냈어

122 I'm not done

못 끝냈어

123 I'm finished working

일 끝냈어

124 It's 90 percent finished

90% 정도 끝냈어

125 We're almost there

거의 다 됐어, 거의 끝났어

126 We're almost finished

거의 다 마쳤어

127 We'd like to wrap this up today

이거 오늘 끝내자고

128 Let's finish it up

이거 끝내자

7 결정과 검토하기

129 I'd like to think it over

생각 좀 해볼게요

130 Let me think it over a little longer

좀 더 생각 좀 해볼게요

131 It's under review

검토 중이야

132 I'll give you an answer after giving it some thought

생각 좀 해보고 답줄게

133 I'll give you an answer after I've talked with my manager

상사와 논의 후 답줄게

134 I don't have the authority to do that

그렇게 할 권한이 없어요

135 I don't have the authority to decide on this matter

이 건에 대한 결정권이 없어요

136 I can't do something like that without discussing it with my superiors

상사와 토의없이 그런 걸 할 수는 없어요

137 I have to talk it over with the boss

사장과 그 문제를 이야기해봐야 돼

138 Let me check with my superiors

상사분들과 확인해볼게요

139 You'd better check with the boss

사장에게 확인해봐요

140 You'd better run it by the boss

사장과 상의해봐요

141
We're waiting for a decision from the people upstairs

윗분들 결정 기다리고 있어

142
The boss refuses to give it his OK

사장이 승낙하지 않고 있어

143
I can't say for sure right now

지금 당장 확실히 말씀 못 드려요

144
It requires a detailed analysis

세부적인 분석이 필요해요

145
Do you need an answer right now?

지금 당장 답변이 필요해요?

146
I'll give you a firm answer by Friday

금요일까지 확실한 대답을 줄게요

147
Thank you for your quick decision

빠른 결정을 해줘 감사해요

148
I'm going with it

난 그것으로 할게요

149 It's now or never

지금 아니면 안돼

150 The sooner, the better

빠를수록 좋아

151 It's all or nothing

모 아니면 도야

---

8 담당자나 책임자에 관한 이야기들

152 Who is in charge?

누가 책임자야?

153 I'm in charge of the project

내가 이 일의 책임자입니다

154 Who calls the shots?

누가 결정권자야?

155 I'm calling the shots

내가 결정해

156 That's[It's] your call

네가 결정할 문제야, 네 뜻에 따를게

157 You decide

네가 결정해

158 You must decide

네가 결정해야 해

159 It's up to you

네가 결정할 일이야

160 It's your choice

네가 선택하는거야

161 The choice is up to you

선택은 너한테 달렸어

162 You're the boss

분부만 내리십시오, 맘대로 하세요

163 You're the doctor

네 조언에 따를게

9 힘드니까 좀 쉬었다고 하자고 말할 때

164 **Let's take a break**

좀 쉽시다

165 **Let's break for coffee**

쉬면서 커피 한잔 합시다

166 **I need some rest**

좀 쉬어야겠어

167 **I need a day off**

하루 쉬어야 되겠어

168 **He has a day off**

그 사람은 오늘 하루 쉬어요

169 **I need to take a day off**

하루 좀 쉬어야겠어

170 **How about going out for a drink tonight?**

오늘 밤 한잔하러 나가자?

171 **Let's go have a drink together tonight**

오늘 밤 함께 한잔 하자

Let's have a drink

한잔 하자

10 일이 많아 바쁘고 지친다고 말하기

173

I've got so much to do

할 일이 많아

174

I have so much to do

할 일이 많아

175

I have many things to do

할 일이 많아

176

I have a lot to do

할 일이 많아

177

There's a lot of work piled up on my desk

내 책상에 할 일이 쌓여있어

178

I'm tied up all day

하루 온종일 꼼짝달싹 못하고 있다

179 I'm tied up with something urgent
급한 일로 꼼짝달싹 못해

180 I'm tied up at the moment
지금 바빠서 꼼짝도 못해

181 I'm not available
바쁘다, 시간이 안돼

182 I'm swamped (with work)
나 (일이) 엄청 바빠

183 I had a pretty hectic day
정신없이 바빴어

184 I'm busy with a client
손님 때문에 바빠요

185 I kept myself busy
그동안 바빴어

186 I don't have time to breathe
숨쉴 시간도 없어

187
I don't (even) have time to catch my breath
숨쉴 겨를이 없어

188
My hands are full right now
지금 무척 바빠

189
I've got my hands full with the work I'm doing now
지금 일로 무척 바빠

190
I'm totally burned out
완전히 뻗었어

191
I'm tired[worn] out
녹초가 됐어

192
I'm stressed out
스트레스로 피곤해

Chapter 08

193
I'm exhausted
지쳤어

194
I'm so beat
지쳤다

195 I'm burned out
난 완전히 기운이 소진됐어

196 I'm wiped out
완전히 뻗었어

11 능력이 안되서 못한다고 말하기

197 I can't do this
나 이건 못해

198 I'm not very good at promoting myself
나 자신을 홍보하는데 서툴러

199 I'm bad at accounting
회계에 약해

200 I'm hopeless with machines
난 기계치야

201 I'm allergic to things like computers
컴퓨터 같은거에 앨러지가 있어

202 I don't know the first thing about computers

컴퓨터의 컴자도 몰라

203 It's far beyond my ability

내 능력 밖이야

204 I'll never get through this

난 절대 못해낼거야

205 I don't feel up to it

내 능력으론 안돼

206 It's not up to that yet

아직 그정도는 안돼요

207 I can't handle all this work on my own

나 혼자 이 일을 다 처리할 수 없어

208 I'm afraid it's more than I can manage

내가 할 수 있는 것 이상인 것 같아

209 I don't stand a chance

난 가능성이 없어

210 **He doesn't have what it takes, does he?**

걔는 자질이 없어, 그지?

211 **I got cold feet**

나 자신없어

212 **That's easy for you to say**

그렇게 말하긴 쉽지

213 **That's easier said than done**

행동보단 말이 쉽지

12 **능력이 돼서 할 수 있다고 자신감있게 말하기**

214 **I can do that[it, this]**

내가 할 수 있어

215 **I can do it better**

내가 더 잘 할 수 있어

216 **Let me take care of it**

나한테 맡겨

217 I'll take over now

이제 내가 책임지고 할게요

218 You can count on me

나한테 맡겨

219 I'm counting on you

난 널 믿고 있어

220 Leave it to me

나한테 맡겨, 내가 할게

221 He's very good at arithmetic

걘 계산에 능해

222 He's good with numbers[computers]

걘 숫자[컴퓨터]에 강해

223 He's familiar with all phases of this business

걘 이 사업의 전 단계를 잘 알아

224 Let me handle it[this]

내가 처리하죠

225
All in all, I feel he's the best choice
종합해 볼 때 걔가 최고의 선택인 것 같아

226
He's the man you want
쟤는 네가 찾던 사람야

227
She's cut out for this job
쟨 이 일에 타고 났어

228
Can you manage?
할 수 있겠어?

229
It's much easier than you think
네가 생각하는 거보다 훨씬 쉬워

230
It's a cinch(= It's a piece of cake)
거저 먹기야

13 잘 나가고 있다고 말해보기

231
I made it!
해냈어!

232 He made it big

걔는 크게 해냈어

233 You made it!

너 해냈구나!

234 I did it!

해냈어!

235 You did it!

해냈구나!

236 You win

내가 졌어

237 I won

내가 이겼어

238 You're a loser

넌 패자야, 멍청이야

239 You got me beat

나보다 낫네

240 You've got me

나도 몰라

241 She is on a roll

그 여자 한창 잘나가고 있어

242 Now there you have me

그건 정확한 지적이야, 내가 졌어, 모르겠어

243 I've got to hand it to you!

너 정말 대단하구나!, 나 너한테 두손 들었다!

244 It works!

제대로 되네!, 효과가 있네!

245 It worked!

됐어!

246 I'm making (some) money

돈을 좀 벌고 있어

247 I'm making money hand over fist

돈을 왕창 벌고 있어

248
I made a killing
떼돈 벌었어

249
Show me the money
돈을 벌어다 줘

250
Money talks
돈으로 안되는 일 없지

251
I'm broke
빈털터리야

252
I have no money
돈이 없어

253
I don't have much money on me now
지금 수중에 돈이 많이 없어

254
I'm out of money[cash]
현금이 없어

255
I'm a little short of money now
지금 현금이 좀 부족해

Chapter

09

숫자 · 연애

상황별 영어
대표문장

Common
Sentences
in Situation
English

01 숫자영어

1 각종 숫자를 영어로 말해보기

001 I got a score of 87.5(eighty-seven point five) percent

87.5점 받았어

002 I usually wear size 9 1/2(nine and a half)

보통 9와 2분의 1사이즈를 신어

003 I saved five times as much as I did last year

작년보다 5배나 저축했어

004 I think it's about 4.5[four point five] meters long

4.5 미터쯤 될거예요

005 He was born in 1985

1985년에 태어났어

006 In the early '90s(nineties)

90년대 초반에요

007 What're you planning to do on the 31st of December?

12/31일에 뭐 할 거야?

008 She's in her early twenties

그녀는 20대 초반야

009 Here we are, sir. That'll be $4.50

다 왔습니다. 손님. 4달러 50센트입니다

010 It's area code four, one, six, two, two, five, double oh, four, one

지역번호 416에 225-0041야

011 It's 010-741-8529

010-741-8529입니다

012 It's Jero_[underline]t@aol.com

제로 언더라인 티 앳 에이오엘 닷컴야

013 What time is it now?

지금 몇시야?

Chapter 09

014 Do you have the time?

몇시야?

015 What time have you got?

몇시야?

016 It's five twenty-four

5시 24분

017 It's ten to two

10시 2분야

018 It's five after[past] one

1시 5분야

019 The clock is five minutes slow[behind]

시계가 5분 늦어

020 The clock is five minutes fast

시계가 5분 빨리가

021 It's 37°(thirty-seven degrees) celsius and sunny

37도고 화창해

2 스포츠 경기 결과를 말해보기

022
Manchester United won five to three
맨체스터 유나이티드가 5대 3로 이겼어

023
Can you believe Chicago White Sox crushed the Yankees by a score of five to zero?
시카고 화이트삭스가 양키스를 5대 0으로 묵사발냈다는 것이 믿기지 않아

024
We're winning by two goals
우리가 두골차로 이기고 있어

025
Colorado is leading by two points
콜로라도가 2점차로 이기고 있어

026
The Red Sox lost five to four
보스톤이 5대 4로 졌어

027
They won by four points
4점차로 이겼어

028
The Jets beat the Flames seven to five
젯츠가 플레임즈를 7:5로 이겼어

029 Giants by five

자이언츠가 5점차로 이겼어

030 They were ahead at halftime

그들이 전반전에 이기고 있었어

031 3-2[three two] with 15 minutes to go

15분 남겨놓고 3대 2로 이기고 있어

032 It ended in a one-one draw

1:1로 끝났어

033 Their players didn't try hard enough, and they lost

열심히 안뛰더니 지더라고

034 She just couldn't turn it around

다시 뒤집지를 못했어

035 Ji-yai Shin is five strokes behind the leader

신지애가 선두와 5타 뒤져

036 Michelle had an impressive round of golf today

미셸이 오늘 골프를 인상적으로 쳤어

상황별 영어
대표문장

02 데이트

3 남녀가 데이트를 하다

037 He's really my type

걘 딱 내 타입이야

038 You're my type

넌 내 타입야

039 He is Mr. Right

걘 내 이상형이야

040 The right woman is just waiting for you

네 연분이 널 기다리고 있다구

041 You're the right girl for me

넌 내 이상형야

042 What type of man[woman] do you like?

어떤 남재[여자]를 좋아해?

043 May I ask you out?

데이트 신청해도 돼요?

044 Would you go on a date with me?

나와 데이트 할래요?

045 Are you asking me out?

데이트 신청하는거야?

046 Are you asking me for a date?

데이트 하자고 하는거야?

047 Are you asking me out on a date?

데이트 신청하는거야?

048 He's going out with Jane

그 사람은 제인하고 사귀는 중이야

049 Are you seeing someone?

누구 사귀는 사람 있어?

050 Are you dating anyone now?

지금 사귀는 사람 있어?

051 Are you going steady with someone?

애인 있어?

052

I'm seeing her

난 그녀하고 사귀고 있어

053

I'm not seeing anybody

난 지금 사귀는 사람 없어

054

I'm just flirting

좀 추근거린 것뿐이야, 작업 좀 들어간 것뿐인데

055

Are you coming on to me?

지금 날 유혹하는거예요?

056

Are you trying to seduce me?

날 유혹하는거야?

057

Are you hitting on me?

지금 날 꼬시는거야?

058

He made a move on me

그 사람 내게 추근대던데

059

He made a pass at me

그 남자가 나한테 수작을 걸었어

상황별 영어
대표문장

COMMON
SENTENCES
IN SITUATION
ENGLISH

03 사랑

4 상대방에게 좋다고 사랑한다고 말할 때

060 **I'm crazy about you**

난 너한테 빠져있어

061 **I'm nuts[mad] about you**

널 미친듯이 좋아해

062 **I've got a crush on you**

난 네가 맘에 들어

063 **I think he has a crush on you**

걔가 널 무척 좋아하는 것 같아

064 **I'm so into you**

나 너한테 푹 빠져 있어

065 **I have (strong) feelings for her**

나 쟤한테 마음있어

066 **You've had feelings for me?**

너 나한테 마음있지?

067
He has[got] a thing for her

걘 그 여자를 맘에 두고 있어

068
What do you see in her?

그 여자 뭐가 좋아?, 어디가 좋은거야?

069
What do you see in this guy?

이 사람 어디가 좋은거야?

070
They really hit it off

쟤네들은 바로 좋아하더라고

071
I (really) hit it off with her[him]

난 걔랑 정말 금세 좋아졌어

072
We have chemistry

우린 잘 통해

073
You turn me on

넌 내 맘에 쏘옥 들어, 넌 날 흥분시켜

074
I fell in love with Dick

딕하고 사랑에 빠졌어

075 I'm deeply in love with Jessica

제시카와 깊은 사랑에 빠졌어

076 I can't live without you

너 없이는 못살아

077 I don't want to live without you

너없인 살고 싶지 않아

078 Life isn't worth living without you

너없는 삶은 살가치가 없어

079 You mean everything to me

난 너밖에 없어

080 I can't stop myself from loving you

널 사랑하지 않고는 못배겨

081 I'm happy to have been part of your life

네 삶의 일부가 되어서 기뻐

082 You make me happy

네가 있어 행복해

083 You belong to me
넌 내 소유야

084 You're mine
넌 내꺼야

085 I'm [all] yours
난 네꺼야

086 It was meant to be
운명이었어, 하늘이 정해준거야

087 You're the one for me
넌 내 짝이야

088 I'm dying to see her
걔 보고 싶어 죽겠어

089 I've never felt like this before
이런 기분 처음이야

5 좀 더 구체적으로 사랑하기

090 He made love to me
그 사람과 사랑을 나눴어

091 It was just a one night thing
하룻밤 잔 것뿐이야

092 I want to have a fling
번개 좀 해야겠어

093 How about a quickie?
가볍게 한번 어때?

094 I want to make out with my girlfriend
애인하고 애무하고 싶어

095 I want to have sex with you
너하고 섹스하고 싶어

096 I want to get laid
섹스하고파

097 They're doing it

재네들 그거 한다

098 He got lucky with Julie

걔가 줄리랑 잤대

상황별 영어
대표문장

COMMON
SENTENCES
IN SITUATION
ENGLISH

04 결혼·이혼

6 결혼과 이혼에 관련된 표현 몇 개

099
Will you marry me?

나랑 결혼해줄래?

100
Will you be my wife[husband]?

내 아내[남편]이 되어줄래요?

101
I want to share the rest of my life with you

나의 여생을 당신과 보내고 싶어

102
She wants to start a family

걔는 가정을 꾸미고 싶어해

103
She is not marriage material

그 여자는 결혼상대는 아냐

104
He is not boyfriend material

그 사람은 애인감이 아냐

105
How's your married life?

결혼생활 어때?

106 We're a well-matched couple
우린 잘 어울리는 커플야

107 I'm pregnant
나 임신했어

108 I'm going to have a baby
애를 가질거야

109 I'm expecting
임신중야

110 What did she have?
남자야 여자야?

111 I'm going to break up with you
우리 그만 만나자

112 We're on a break
잠시 떨어져 있는거야

113 I'm over you
너랑은 끝났어

114 I'm through with you
너랑 이제 끝이야

115 I dumped him
내가 걔 찼어

116 We fight a lot
우린 싸움을 많이 해

117 My wife's cheating on me
아내가 바람을 폈어

118 My wife's a two-timer
아내가 바람둥이야

119 I had an affair with my secretary
내가 비서와 바람을 폈어

120 We're living separately now
우린 현재 별거하고 있어

121 I'm separated from my wife
아내와 별거하고 있어

122   I wish I had never met you
널 안 만났더라면 좋았을 텐데

123   I regret meeting you
널 만난 걸 후회해

124   I wish you were never a part of my life
너를 만나지 않았더라면 좋았을 텐데

Common Sentences
in Situation English

Chapter

10

만남 · 약속

01 인사
02 초대·방문
03 약속

상황별 영어
대표문장

COMMON
SENTENCES
IN SITUATION
ENGLISH

01 인사

1 아는 사람을 만났을 때

001
How (are) you doing?
안녕?, 잘 지냈어?

002
How are you?
잘 지내?(만났을 때), 괜찮어?(상대방에게 괜찮냐고 물어볼 때)

003
How's it going?
잘 지내?

004
How's it going today?
오늘 어때?

005
How's everything going?
다 잘돼 가?

006
What's new?
뭐 새로운 일 있어?

007
What's new with you?
그러는 넌 별일 없어?

What's new?라고 묻는 상대방의 인사에 답하는 전형적인 인사.

008 ## What's up?

어때?

009 ## What's happening?

어떻게 지내?, 잘 지내니?

010 ## What's going on?

무슨 일이야?

011 ## What's going on in there[here]?

거기[여기] 무슨 일 있어?

012 ## What's going on with him?

그 사람 무슨 일 있어?

013 ## (You) Doing okay?

잘지내?, 괜찮어?

014 ## (Is) Everything okay?

잘 지내지?, 일은 다 잘 되지?

015 ## (Have) (you) Been okay?

그동안 잘 지냈어?

016 How're you getting along?

어떻게 지내?

017 How's the[your] family?

가족들은 다 잘 지내?

018 How's the wife[your kid]?

부인[애들]은 잘 지내?

019 How's business?

일은 어때?

2 오래간만에 아는 사람을 만났을 때

020 How (have) you been?

어떻게 지냈어?, 잘 지냈어?

021 What have you been up to?

뭐하고 지냈어?, 별일 없어?

022 What have you been doing?

뭐하고 지냈어?

023 Long time no see

오랜만이야

024 It's been a long time

오랜간만이야

025 I haven't seen you for a long time[for ages]

오랜만이야

026 What're you doing here?

여긴 어쩐 일이야?

027 Fancy meeting you here

이런 데서 다 만나다니

028 Look who's here!

아니 이게 누구야!

029 I didn't expect to see you here

여기서 널 만날 줄 생각도 못했어

030 I never thought I'd see you here

여기서 널 만날 줄 생각도 못했어

Chapter **10**

031 ## Are you here on business?

여기 비즈니스로 온거야?

032 ## What's the story?

어떻게 지내?

033 ## How's life[the world] treating you?

사는 건 어때?

034 ## Nice weather, huh?

날씨 좋으네 그지?

3 그밖의 인사표현

035 ## How was your day?

오늘 어땠어?

036 ## How are you feeling?

기분 어때?

037 ## Where're you headed?

어디 가?

038 Where're you going?

어디 가?

039 Where're you off to?

어디 가?

040 What're you doing?

뭐해?

041 Where have you been?

어디 갔었어?

042 I ran into her

그 여자와 우연히 마주쳤어

043 I keep bumping into you

우리 자꾸 마주치네요

4 특별한 날에 하는 인사법

044 Happy birthday!

생일 축하해!

045 Happy New Year!

새해 복많이 받아!

046 Happy New Year to you, too!

너도 새해 복많이 받아!

047 (You) Have a Merry Christmas!

메리 크리스마스!

048 I wish you a Merry Christmas!

성탄절 즐겁게 보내!

049 Happy holidays!

휴일 잘 보내!

050 Happy Valentine's Day!

발렌타인 잘 보내!

051 Happy Thanksgiving!

추석 잘 보내!

052 Happy Chusok!

추석 잘 지내!

5 뭔가 심상치 않을 때

053
What's wrong (with you)?
무슨 일이야?, 뭐 잘못됐어?

054
What's the problem?
무슨 일인데?

055
What's the matter with you?
무슨 일이야?, 도대체 왜그래?

056
What happened?
무슨 일이야?, 어떻게 된 거야?

057
What happened to[with] you?
너 무슨 일이야?, 왜 그래?

058
What's with you?
뭐 땜에 그래?

059
What's with your hair?
머리가 왜 그래?

COMMON
SENTENCES
IN SITUATION
ENGLISH

060 What's with her[him, the guys]?

쟤(들) 왜 저래?

061 What's gotten into you?

뭣 때문에 이러는거야?

062 What's gotten into your head?

무슨 생각으로 그래?

063 What's cooking?

무슨 일이야?

064 What's eating you?

뭐가 문제야?, 무슨 걱정거리라도 있어?

065 What gives?

무슨 일 있어?

066 Why the long face?

왜 그래?, 무슨 기분 안좋은 일 있어?

067 What's bothering you?

뭐가 잘못됐어?

068
What's on your mind?
왜 그래?, 문제가 뭔대?

069
Do you have something on your mind?
왜 그래?

070
What are you up to?
뭐해?, 뭘 할거야?

071
I know what you're up to
네 속셈 다 알아

6 상대방이 좋아 보일 때

072
Look at you!
얘 좀 봐라!, (어머) 얘 좀 봐!

상대방이 멋진 차림을 하였거나 혹은 바람직한 행동을 했을 경우 혹은 어처구니 없는 행동을 한 상대방을 향해 비난하면서도 쓰인다.

073
You look good[great]!
너 멋져 보인다!

074
You haven't changed at all
너 하나도 안 변했네

074 You haven't changed much

너 별로 안 변했어

075 You've really changed

너 정말 많이 변했다

076 You've grown up

너 많이 컸다

078 Are you gaining weight?

살쪘어?

079 Are you getting fatter?

뚱뚱해졌어?

080 Are you losing weight?

살 빠졌어?

7 상대방이 안 좋아 보일 때

081 You don't look good today

오늘 너 안 좋아 보여

082
You look serious
너 심각해 보여

083
You seem nervous
너 초조해 보여

084
Something's wrong with you today
너 오늘 좀 이상해

085
You look depressed
너 매우 지쳐보여

086
You look sad, today
너 오늘 슬퍼보여

087
You look exhausted
너 지쳐보인다

088
You look very tired
너 매우 피곤해 보여

089
You need a break
너 좀 쉬어야 돼

8 상대방의 인사에 잘 지내고 있다고 말하기

090
I'm doing OK
잘 지내고 있어

091
I'm fine. How about you?
잘 지내. 넌 어때?

092
I'm cool
잘 지내

093
Not bad
그리 나쁘지 않아

094
Pretty good
잘 지내

095
(It) Couldn't be better
최고야. 아주 좋아

096
Things have never been better
최고야

097 (Things) Could be better

별로야, 그냥 그래

Could be better는 '더 좋을 수도 있는데 그렇지 않다'라는 의미로 다소 부정적인 표현인 반면 다음의 Could be worse는 '더 나쁠 수도 있는데 그렇지 않다'라는 의미로 다소 긍정적인 표현임.

098 Could be worse

그럭저럭 잘 지내지

099 I couldn't ask for more

최고야, 더 이상 바랄 게 없어

100 (I) Can't complain

잘 지내

101 (I have) Nothing to complain about

잘 지내

102 No complaints

잘 지내

103 Not (too) much

별일 없어, 그냥 그럭저럭

104
Nothing much

별로 특별한 건 없어, 별일 아냐

105
So so

그저 그래

106
Nothing special

별일 아냐, 별일 없어

107
Nothing in particular

별일 아냐

108
Same as always

맨날 똑같지 뭐

109
Same as usual

늘 그렇지 뭐

110
Same old story[stuff]

늘 그렇지 뭐

111
Not very well

안 좋아

112
Not good

안 좋아

113
Not so great

좋지 않아

9 사람들 만나서 소개할 때

114
Hello, my name is David

안녕하세요, 데이빗이라고 합니다

115
I'd like to introduce myself

제 소개를 하겠습니다

116
I'd like you to meet a friend of mine

내 친구 한 명 소개할게

117
I want you to meet Sam

샘하고 인사해

118
Paul, meet Jane

폴, 제인이야

119 Mina, this is Peter...Peter, Mina

미나, 이쪽이 피터야… 피터, 이쪽은 미나야

120 Mr.Kim, this is Mr.Johnson, my boss

미스터 김, 이분은 사장님인 존슨 씨야

121 Mary, have you met Dan?

메리야, 댄 만나본 적 있니?

122 Tom, Laura is the girl I was telling you about

탐, 얘가 내가 말하던 로라야

123 I've heard so much[a lot] about you

네 얘기 많이 들었어

124 Just call me John

그냥 존이라고 불러

125 You can call me by my first name

이름으로 불러

126 Who's this?

이 사람 누구야?

¹²⁷ Do you know each other?

둘이 아는 사이니?

¹²⁸ Have you two met before?

너희 둘 전에 만난 적 있어?

¹²⁹ Don't I know you from somewhere?

어디서 만난 적 있지 않나요?

¹³⁰ We've never met before

우린 초면야

¹³¹ I don't think we've met before

초면인 것 같은데요

¹³² May I have your name, please?

이름 좀 알려줄래요?

🔟 만나서 반갑다고, 반가웠다고 말하기

¹³³ Nice to meet you

만나서 반가워요

134 (It's) Nice to see you

만나서 반가워요, 만나서 반가웠어요

135 It's great seeing you again

다시 만나 반가워

136 I'm happy to see you

만나서 반가워

137 I'm glad[pleased] to meet you

만나서 반가워요

138 (It's, It was) Good to see you

만나서 반가워, 만나서 반가웠어

139 Good to see you again

다시 만나니 반가워

140 Good to see you too

나도 만나서 반가워

141 (It was) Nice meeting you

만나서 반가웠어

142 Nice talking to you

만나서 반가웠어

11 잠시 자리를 비울 때

143 I'll be back

다녀 올게, 금방 올게

144 (I'll) Be right back

바로 올게

145 (I'll) Be back soon

금방 돌아올게

146 (I'll) Be back in a sec

곧 돌아올게

147 (I'll) Be back in just a minute

금세 돌아올게

148 She'll be back any minute

그 여자는 곧 돌아올거예요

149 I'll be right with you

잠시만, 곧 돌아올게

150 I'll be with you in a sec[minute]

곧 돌아올게

151 Can[Could] you excuse us?

실례 좀 해도 될까요?, 자리 좀 비켜주시겠어요?

152 Could[May] I be excused?

이만 일어나도 될까요?, 실례 좀 해도 되겠어요?

12 그만 가봐야 된다고 일어서기(1)

153 I have (got) to go

이제 가봐야겠어, 이제 (전화를) 끊어야겠어

154 I'd better go now

이젠 가야겠어

155 I have to go to a wedding

결혼식에 가야돼

I have to go to + 장소 …에 가야 해. I have to go to 다음에 동사가 오면 「…하러 가야 돼」라는 의미가 된다.

156 I'm really sorry but I have to go to work

미안하지만 일하러가야 돼요.

157 I have to leave

출발해야겠어

158 Let's leave

가자, 출발하자

159 I must be going

그만 가봐야 될 것 같아

160 I think I'd better be going

그만 가봐야 될 것 같아

161 It's getting late and I'd better be going

늦어서 가봐야 돼

162 It's time we should be going

그만 일어납시다

163 I should get going

서둘러 가봐야겠어

Chapter 10

164 **I'd better get going**

가보는 게 좋겠어

165 **I've got to get going**

가야겠어

166 **Let's get going**

이젠 어서 가자

167 **I('ve) got to get moving**

가봐야겠어

169 **You'd better get moving**

너 그만 가봐야지

169 **(It's) Time for me to go**

갈 시간이야, 일어서야겠어

170 **Time to move**

갈 시간이야

171 **Let's hit the road**

출발하자고

13 그만 가봐야 된다고 일어서기(2)

172
I'm going to take off
그만 일어서야겠어

173
I must be off
이제 가봐야겠어

174
(I'd) Better be off
가봐야겠어

175
I'd better be going
가봐야겠어

176
I am off (now)
나 간다

177
I'm off to Jeff's
제프네 집에 가려구

178
I'm off to see your dad
너희 아빠 만나러 갈래 (be off to + 동사)

179 I've got to run
서둘러 가봐야겠어

180 (I've) Got to fly
난 이만 사라져야겠어

181 I'm out of here
나 갈게

182 I'm not here
나 여기 없는거야

183 I'm gone
나 간다

184 I'm getting out of here
나 간다, 지금 나 갈건데

185 Let's get out of here
나가자, 여기서 빠져 나가자

186 I'm leaving. Bye!
나 간다. 안녕!

187 Are you leaving so soon?

벌써 가려구?, 왜 이렇게 빨리 가?

188 I don't want to wear out my welcome

넘 번거롭게 하는게 아닌지 모르겠네

189 I wish I could stay longer

더 남아 있으면 좋을 텐데

190 You're excused

그러세요, 괜찮다, 그만 나가 보거라

191 You're dismissed

가도 좋아, 해산

192 Class dismissed

수업 끝났습니다

14 나중에 다시 보자고 하면서 헤어지기

193 See you later

나중에 봐

194 ## (I'll) See you guys later

얘들아 나중에 봐

195 ## I'll try to see you later

나중에 봐

196 ## (I'll) Be seeing you

또 보자

197 ## See you soon

또 보자

198 ## See you around

또 보자

199 ## See you in the morning[tomorrow]

아침에[내일] 보자

200 ## I'll see you then

그럼 그때 보자

201 ## Catch you later

나중에 보자

202 I'll catch up with you in the gym

체육관에서 보자

203 I'll catch up with you later

나중에 보자

204 I'll try to catch you some other time

언제 한번 보도록 하자

205 Goodbye for now

그만 여기서 작별하죠

206 Bye for now

그만 여기서 헤어지자

207 Goodbye until next time

다시 만날 때까지 잘 있어

208 Bye Jane!

제인아 잘가!

209 Bye-bye!

안녕!

Chapter 10

210 Don't work too hard

너무 무리하지 말구

211 Take care!

조심하고!

212 Take care of yourself

몸조심해

213 Be careful

조심해

214 Ciao!

잘 가!

215 Sayonara!

잘 가!

216 Hasta la vista!

잘 가, 또 보자!

15 상대방에게 행운을 빌어주면서

217 # Have a nice day

오늘 잘 지내

218 # Have a nice weekend

주말 잘 보내

219 # Have a nice trip!

여행 멋지게 보내고!

220 # Have fun!

재미있게 보내!

221 # Enjoy yourself!

즐겁게 지내!

222 # Good luck

행운을 빌어

223 # Good luck with that!

행운이 있기를!

224 **(The) Best of luck (to someone)!**

잘 되기를 빌게!

225 **I wish you success!**

성공하길 빌어!

226 **Good luck, go get them**

행운을 빌어, 가서 잡으라고

227 **Good luck (to you), you'll need it**

행운을 빌어, 행운이 필요할거야

228 **My fingers are crossed**

행운을 빌어요

229 **I'll keep my fingers crossed (for you)!**

행운을 빌어줄게!

230 **Lucky me**

나한테 다행이구만

231 **Lucky bastard!**

그놈의 자식 운도 좋구만!

239 Could I see you again?

다시 한번 볼 수 있어?

240 Don't stay away so long

자주 좀 와

241 Give me a call sometime

한번 전화해

242 Call me later

나중에 전화해

243 I wish I could go with you

너랑 같이 가면 좋을텐데

244 Let's get[keep] in touch!

연락하고 지내자!

245 Don't forget to e-mail me

잊지말고 메일 보내

246 Don't forget to write

잊지말고 편지 써

247 Drop me a line

나한테 편지 좀 써

248 Give my best to your folks

가족들에게 안부 전해줘

249 All the best to everyone

모두에게 안부 전해줘

250 Please give my regards to your family

가족에게 안부 전해줘

251 Say hello[hi] to your wife

부인에게 안부 전해 주게나

COMMON
SENTENCES
IN SITUATION
ENGLISH

상황별 영어
대표문장

초대·방문

17 집이나 파티에 초대하기

252
Come over to my place[house]

우리 집에 들려

253
Please come to John's farewell party this Friday

금요일 존 송별회에 와

254
Please attend our office party

회사 회식에 참석해요

255
Drop by for a drink

언제 한번 놀러 와 한잔 하자고

256
If you're ever in Seoul, do drop by

서울에 오게 되면 들리라고

257
Drop by sometime

언제 한번 들려

swing by~라고 해도 된다.

258
You're invited to Bob's bachelor party

밥의 총각파티에 참석했으면 해

259
We cordially invite you to attend the wedding
결혼식에 참석해줬으면 해요

260
Hope you can make it
너도 올 수 있으면 좋겠어

261
Hope you can come
네가 올 수 있기를 바래

262
I'm sorry I can't make it
미안하지만 못가

263
When can I come over?
내가 언제 갈까?

264
When can I stop by?
내가 언제 들를까?

265
When can you come over?
언제 올 수 있어?

18 방문하거나 방문한 사람에게 누구냐고 물어볼 때

266
Hello, is anyone there?
여보세요?, 아무도 안계세요?

267
Is anyone here?
누구 안 계세요?

268
(Hello) Anybody home?
누구 집에 없어요?, 안 계세요?

269
I'd like to see Mr.James
제임스 씨를 만나뵈려고요

270
I came[am] here to see Mr. Smith
스미스 씨를 만나뵈러 왔어요

271
Who is it?
누구세요?, 누구야?

272
Who's there?
누구세요?

273
Who was it?
누군데? 누구였어?

274 Would you get that?

문 좀 열어줄래?, 전화 좀 받아줄래?

275 Could you answer it for me?

대신 좀 열어[받아]줄래?

276 I'll get it

내가 받을게

277 Let me

내가 받을게

278 I'm home

나 왔어

279 Come on in

어서 들어와

280 Please come in

어서 들어와

281 Welcome home

어서 와

282 Welcome!

어서 와!

283 Welcome to our Christmas party

크리스마스 파티에 오신 걸 환영합니다

284 Welcome aboard

함께 일하게 된 걸 환영해, 귀국[귀항]을 축하해

285 Won't you come in?

들어오지 않을래?

286 It's nice to be here

저도 여기 오게 돼서 기뻐요

287 It's great to be here

여기 오게 돼 무척 기뻐요

19 와줘서 고맙다고 말하기

288 I'm glad you could come

네가 와줘서 기뻐

289

How nice of you to come

와줘서 고마워

290

Thank you for coming

와줘서 고마워

291

Thank you[Thanks] for inviting me

초대해줘서 고마워

292

I really like your apartment

너희 아파트 정말 좋다

293

Can I park my car here?

여기 주차해도 돼?

294

Is parking okay here?

여기 주차해도 괜찮어?

295

Is it all right to park my car here?

차 여기다 주차해도 돼?

296

Have[Take] a seat

앉아

297 **Please sit down**

앉으세요

298 **Make yourself at home**

편히계세요

299 **Please feel free to make yourself at home**

집처럼 편히 하세요

300 **Please make yourself comfortable**

편히 하세요

301 **Make yourself a drink and relax**

술 한 잔 따라 마시며 편히 쉬어

302 **May I use your rest room?**

화장실 좀 써도 될까요?

303 **May I use your bathroom[toilet]?**

화장실 좀 써도 될까요?

304 **Where's the bathroom?**

화장실이 어디예요?

305

How can I get to the bathroom?

화장실 어떻게 가죠?

Common
Sentences
in Situation
English

상황별 영어
대표문장

약속

20 상대방에게 시간이 있냐고 물어보기

306
(You) Got a minute?
시간돼?

307
Do you have (some) time?
시간 있어요?

308
Are you available on Thursday morning?
목요일 오전에 시간 돼?

309
Are you available after the meeting for lunch?
회의 후에 점심 가능해?

310
Are you available?
시간돼?

311
Will you be free to go to the movies on the weekend?
주말에 영화보러 갈 수 있어?

Will you be free to + 동사 ? …할 시간이 돼?

312 Are you free in the afternoon?

오후에 시간 있어?

313 Do you have time to talk for a bit?

잠깐 얘기할 시간이 있나요?

Do you have time to + 동사 ? …할 시간이 있어요?

314 Do you have time to see me on the weekend?

주말에 만날 수 있을까?

315 Let's get together (sometime)

(조만간) 한번 보자

316 Why don't we get together on Wednesday?

수요일에 만날까요?

317 Let's meet to talk about it

만나서 그 얘기해보자

318 I'd like to meet with you after work if you're not too busy

바쁘지 않으면 퇴근후 봤으면 해

319 I wonder if we could get together on the 15th

15일에 만날 수 있을까

320 Shall we get together on Thursday after five?

목요일 5시 이후에 볼래요?

321 Are you doing anything this afternoon?

오후에 뭐 계획있어?

322 Okay, let me check my schedule

일정을 한번 확인해 보죠

323 I'd like to set up an appointment for Monday

월요일로 약속정하고 싶어요

324 Can you make time to discuss our purchases?

시간내서 구매품 의논할 수 있어?

21 언제 어디서 만날지 정할 때

325 How about tomorrow morning?

내일 오전이 어때?

How about + 구체적인 장소/시간 ? ···가 어때?

326 How about Friday in my office?

금요일날 내 사무실에서 어때?

327 About what time?

몇시에?

328 Would this afternoon be all right with you?

오늘 오후 괜찮겠어요?

Is + 시간 + all right? …가 괜찮아?

329 When can you make it?

몇시에 도착할 수 있겠니?

make it은 'to arrive in time'이란 의미로 「약속 시간에 닿다」라는 의미.

330 Can you make it?

올 수 있어?

331 Can you make it at 7?

7시에 올 수 있겠니?

332 When and where can I meet you?

언제 어디서 만날까?

333 What time is[would be] good for you?

몇시가 좋겠어?

334 **When is good for you?**

언제가 좋아?

335 **What time would you like to meet?**

몇시에 만날래?

336 **When is the most convenient time for you?**

언제가 가장 편리한 시간야?

337 **Does this afternoon work for you?**

오후에 괜찮으세요?

338 **That works for me**

나도 그때가 괜찮아요.

339 **You decide when**

언제 만날지 네가 결정해

340 **You decide where**

어디서 만날지 네가 결정해

341 **That'll be fine. See you then**

그게 좋겠군요. 그때 봐요

Whenever you're free

네가 시간나면 아무때나

Whenever

아무 때나

When you have time

네가 시간될 때

Anytime is fine

아무 때나 좋아

22 약속을 거절하거나 연기하기

I'll take a rain check

이번에는 다음으로 미룰게

Do you mind if I take a rain check?

다음으로 미뤄도 될까?

Maybe some other time

다음을 기약하지

349 We'll try again some other time

나중을 기약하자

350 I have no time available this week

이번 주엔 시간낼 수가 없어

351 I have no time to see you in the afternoon

오후에 만날 시간이 없어

352 I'm afraid I have another appointment

미안하지만 선약이 있어

353 I have another appointment at that time

그 시간에는 선약이 있는데요

354 That's a bad day for me

그날은 안되는데

355 Sorry, I won't be able to make it this weekend

미안 주말 약속 못 지켜

356 I won't be able to make it to the presentation

발표회에 못가

357 I won't be able to make it
못갈 것 같아

358 Could we change it to Monday?
월요일로 바꿀 수 있어?

359 I'd rather make it later if that's okay
괜찮다면 날짜를 더 미루는게 낫겠어요

360 I'm afraid I have to cancel tomorrow's appointment
내일 약속 취소해야 돼

361 I'll be there
갈게

362 I'll be right there
곧 갈게, 지금 가

363 I'm going to be there
갈게, 갈거야

364 You bet I'll be there
꼭 갈게

365 She's going to be here

개는 여기 올거야

366 I'm going to make it to the wedding

결혼식에 갈 예정이야

367 I'm going

나 가

368 I'm not going

나 안가

23 약속시간에 늦거나 못온다고 말하기

369 I'm sorry but I'm going to be a little late

미안하지만 좀 늦을 것 같아

370 I might be about thirty minutes late

한 30분 정도 늦을 것 같아

371 I'm sorry I'm late

늦어서 미안해

372 Something's come up

일이 좀 생겼어

373 Something unexpected came up

갑자기 일이 생겨서요

374 What time do you think you will show up?

몇시에 올 수 있을 것 같아?

375 I'll be there soon

곧 갈게

376 I'll try and get there as soon as I can

가능한 한 빨리 가도록 할게

377 I'm sorry I kept you waiting so long

너무 오래 기다리게 해서 미안해요

378 I'm sorry to have kept you waiting for so long

넘 오래 기다리게 해서 미안

379 How long have you been waiting?

얼마동안 기다린거야?

380 Please excuse me for being late

늦어서 미안해

381 I apologize for being so late

늦어서 죄송해요

382 What took you so long?

뭣 때문에 이렇게 오래 걸렸어?

383 I don't know what's keeping her

걔가 뭣 때문에 늦는지 모르겠어

384 I lost track of time

시간이 어떻게 되는 지 몰랐어

385 I got held up at work

일에 잡혀서 말야

386 Everyone's waiting for us

다들 우리를 기다리고 있어

387 You kept me waiting for an hour

한 시간 동안 널 기다렸어

388 You're always late for everything

매사에 항상 늦는구만

Common Sentences
in Situation English

Chapter 11

감사 · 격려

미 감사

1 thank와 appreciate를 이용해 고맙다고 말하기

001

Thank you very[so] much
고마워

002

Thanks a lot
고마워

003

Thank you for the lovely present
선물 고마워

Thank you for + 명사 …에 대해 고마워

004

Thanks a lot for the great meal!
맛있는 식사 고마워!

005

Thank you very much for your help
도와줘서 정말 고마워

006

Thank you for your time
시간내줘서 고마워

007

Thank you for the compliment
칭찬해줘서 고마워

Chapter 11

008

Thank you for your concern

걱정해줘서 고마워

009

Thank you for all you've done

여러모로 고마워

010

Thank you for the help

도와줘서 고마워

011

Thank you for giving me another chance

기회를 한 번 더 줘서 고마워

Thank you for ~ ing …해줘서 고마워

012

Thank you for telling me

말해줘서 고마워

013

Thank you for letting me know

알려줘서 고마워

014

Thanks for saying so

그렇게 말해줘서 고마워

015

Thank you anyway

어쨌든 고마워

016 **Thanks anyway, though**

어쨌든 고마워

017 **Thank you in advance**

고맙구만

018 **I really appreciate this**

정말 고마워

019 **I appreciate it**

고마워

020 **I appreciate your help**

도와줘서 감사해요

021 **I appreciate the support**

도와줘서 감사해요

022 **I appreciate your kindness**

친절을 베푸셔서 감사해요

2 또 다른 방법으로 고맙다고 말하기

023 That's very kind of you
정말 친절하군요

024 How kind of you to say so
그렇게 말씀해주시니 정말 친절하네요

025 It's[That's] very nice of you
정말 친절하네요

026 It's very thoughtful of you
사려가 깊으시군요

027 That's so sweet
고맙기도 해라

주로 여성들이 쓰는 말로 주어를 바꿔 This is so sweet, It's so sweet라고 해도 된다.

028 You're so sweet
정말 고마워

029 You're so generous
맘씨가 참 좋으네

030 You're such a kind person

정말 친절하네요

031 You've got such a good heart

넌 무척 자상한 얘야

032 I'm really grateful to you

정말 감사드려요

033 I don't know how to thank you

고마워서 어쩌죠

034 I have no words to thank you

뭐라고 감사해야 할지 모르겠어

035 I can't thank you enough

뭐라 감사하다고 해야 할지

036 I don't know what to say

뭐라고 말해야 할지

037 You shouldn't have done this

이러지 않아도 되는데

038

I'm flattered

그렇게 말해주면 고맙지, 과찬의 말씀을

039

I'm honored

영광인데요

040

It was a great help

큰 도움이 됐습니다

041

You were a great help

정말 많은 도움이 되었어요

042

You've been very helpful

넌 참 도움이 많이 됐어

043

You've been a big[great] help

넌 큰 도움이 되었어

044

I owe it to my colleagues

제 동료 덕이에요

045

I owe you a favor

신세를 졌구만

046 I owe you one

신세가 많구나

047 You saved my life

네 덕택에 살았네

048 How nice!

고마워라!

049 She's very supportive

그 여자는 도움이 많이 되고 있어

050 He's been incredibly supportive of me

그 남자는 날 정말 많이 도와주고 있어

051 God bless you!

이렇게 고마울 수가!

God bless you!는 고맙다는 인사 뿐만 아니라 상대방이 재채기를 할 때 "신의 가호가 있기를" 이라는 의미로 쓰이기도 하는데 이는 재채기를 할 때 혼이 달아난다는 미신 때문에 생긴 표현.

3 상대방이 감사하다고 할 때 괜찮다고 말하기

052 You're welcome

천만에요

강조하려면 You're very welcome, You're quite welcome이라고 하면 된다.

053

Not at all

뭘요

054

Don't mention it

신경쓰지 마요

055

(It's) My pleasure

도움이 됐다니 내가 기쁘네요

056

The pleasure is mine

제가 좋아서 한 일인데요

057

No problem

뭘 그런걸

058

No sweat

뭘 별것도 아닌데

059

Never mind

마음쓰지마

060

(Please) Think nothing of it

마음쓰지마

061

It was nothing

별거 아닌데

062

Don't worry about it

별거 아닌데

063

I'm glad you think so

그렇게 생각한다니 고마워

064

I'm glad I could help

내가 도움이 되서 기뻐

065

I'm sure you would have done the same (in my position)

너도 (내입장이면) 나처럼 했을거야

상황별 영어
대표문장

칭찬·축하

ES
ION

4 상대방에게 잘했다고 칭찬이나 축하를 할 때(1)

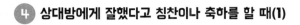

066
(That's) Great!
잘됐다!

067
Excellent!
아주 좋아!

068
Fantastic!
끝내주네!

069
Wonderful!
멋져!

070
You did a good[nice] job!
아주 잘했어!

071
Good for you
잘됐네, 잘했어

072
Good for me
나한테 잘된 일야

073 Lucky for you

잘됐어

074 You deserve it

넌 충분히 그럴만해

075 You more than deserve it

너 정도면 충분히 그럴 자격이 되고도 남아

076 Nice going!

참 잘했어!

077 Well done

잘했어

078 Top notch!

최고야, 훌륭해!

079 There is nothing like that!

저 만한 게 없지!

문맥에 따라서는 단순히 "그와 같은 건 없다"라는 의미로도 쓰인다.

080 Nice move

좋았어, 잘했어

081 Nice try

(하지만) 잘했어

목적을 달성하지 못했지만 그래도 잘했다고 상대방이 한 시도를 칭찬할 때 쓰는 표현.

082 You can't beat that

짱이야, 완벽해

083 Can't top that

끝내준다

084 Congratulations!

축하해!

085 Congratulations on your marriage!

결혼 축하해!

086 Congratulations on your promotion!

승진 축하해!

5 상대방에게 잘했다고 칭찬이나 축하를 할 때(2)

087 You're doing fine!

잘하고 있어!

088 Way to go!

잘한다 잘해!

089 I am happy for you

네가 잘돼서 나도 기쁘다

090 That's the spirit!

바로 그거야

091 That's the stuff

바로 그거야, 잘했어

092 That's the ticket

바로 그거야, 안성맞춤이야, 진심이야

093 It's not that bad

괜찮은데

094 Good boy

잘했어

095 That was very smart

아주 현명했네

096
I envy you
부럽네

097
I knew I could count on you
넌 믿음직해

098
I have confidence in you
난 널 신뢰해

099
I'm depending on you
난 널 의지하고 있어

100
You were great!
너 대단했어!

101
I'm impressed
인상적이야

102
Everyone was really impressed
사람들이 모두 정말 감동했어

103
Give me five
손바닥 부딪히자

104 **It gets two thumbs up**

최고야

105 **Attaboy!**

야 잘했다!

6 한번 해보라고, 할 수 있다고 격려를 할 때

106 **Give it a try!**

한번 해봐!

107 **Just try it!**

한번 해봐!

108 **Try it!**

해봐!

109 **Try again!**

다시 해봐!

110 **Let's give it a try**

한번 해보자

111 **Why don't you try it?**

해보지 그래?, 한번 해봐

112 **Go for it**

한번 시도해봐

113 Let's go for it
한번 시도해보자

114 Give it a shot
한번 해봐

115 Let's give it a shot
한번 해보자

116 Let me have a shot at it
내가 한번 해볼게

117 It can't[won't] hurt to try
한번 해본다고 해서 나쁠 건 없지

118 It wouldn't hurt
해본다고 나쁠 건 없어

119 It doesn't hurt to ask
물어본다고 손해볼 것 없어, 그냥 한번 물어본 거예요

120 You've got nothing to lose
밑져야 본전인데 뭐

121 Nothing to lose

밑질 거 없지

122 I will try my luck

(되든 안되든) 한번 해봐야겠어

123 Get started

시작해봐

124 You can do it

넌 할 수 있어

125 If you try, you can do it

노력하면 넌 할 수 있어

126 Get it together!

잘해봐!

get it together의 의미는 'to be organized and successful in your life, job etc.'이다.

127 You can do anything if you really want to

네가 진정 원한다면 뭐든 다 할 수 있어

7 계속하라고 북돋아 줄 때

128 Keep going!

계속 해!

129 Keep going like this

지금처럼 계속해

130 Get going

계속해

131 Let's keep going

자 계속하자

132 Keep talking

계속 이야기해봐

133 Keep (on) trying

계속 정진해, 멈추지 말고 계속 노력해

134 Carry on

계속해

135 Go on

(어서) 계속해

8 포기하지 말고 기운내라고 말할 때

144 **Don't give up (yet)!**

(아직) 포기하지마!

145 **Never give up!**

절대 포기하지 마

146 **Don't quit trying**

포기하지 마

147 **Don't give up too easily**

너무 쉽게 포기하지마

148 **You (always) give up too easily**

넌 (늘) 너무 쉽게 포기하더라

149 **Cheer up!**

기운 내!, 힘내!

150 **Get your act together**

기운 차려

Chapter 11

151 Pull yourself together
기운 내, 똑바로 잘해

152 Hang in there
끝까지 버텨

153 Stick with it
포기하지마, 계속해

154 Never say die!
기운내!, 약한 소리하지마!

155 Keep your chin up
힘 좀 내

156 Be positive
긍정적으로 생각해

157 Look on[at] the bright side
밝은 면을 보라고

158 You go back out there
다시 뛰어야지

159 You gotta get back in the game

다시 뛰어야지, 다시 한번 싸워야지

160 It's not impossible

불가능한 일은 아니지

161 Don't lose your nerve

자신없어 하지마

162 Don't chicken out

겁먹고 물러서지 마

163 Don't be a chicken[coward]

겁먹지 말라고

미안

9 sorry와 apologize을 이용해 미안하다고 말하기

164 I'm (terribly) sorry

(정말) 미안해

165 I'm so sorry!

정말 미안해!

166 Oh, sorry

어, 미안

167 Oops, so sorry

아이구, 미안해라

168 I'm sorry about that

미안해

169 I'm sorry about the other day

요전날 미안했어.

170 (I'm) Sorry for the inconvenience

불편하게 해서 미안해

미안하게 된 원인을 말하려면 I'm sorry for 다음에 명사 혹은 동사의 ing를 붙이면 된다.

¹⁷¹ I'm sorry to trouble you

귀찮게 해서 미안해

¹⁷² I'm sorry if I caused any trouble

말썽피웠다면 미안해

I'm sorry 다음에 (that) 절 혹은 if 절 등을 붙여 미안한 내용을 말해도 된다.

¹⁷³ I'm sorry it slipped my mind

깜박해서 미안해

¹⁷⁴ I'm sorry I couldn't come

오지 못해서 미안해

¹⁷⁵ You can't believe how sorry I am

내가 얼마나 미안한지 모를거야

¹⁷⁶ I can't tell you how sorry I am

얼마나 미안한지 말로 할 수도 없어

¹⁷⁷ Excuse me

미안해

역시 미안해하는 내용은 Excuse me for 이하에 말하면 된다.

¹⁷⁸ I just want to apologize for that

내 사과할게요

179 **I don't know how to apologize to you**

뭐라 사과해야 할지 모르겠네요

180 **I have no words to apologize to you**

뭐라 사과해야 할지 모르겠어요

181 **Please accept my sincere apologies**

진심어린 사과를 드립니다

182 **I accept your apology**

용서했어요

183 **Please forgive me**

용서해줘

10 **나의 잘못이라고 솔직히 말하기**

184 **It was my mistake**

내 잘못이야

185 **My mistake**

내 잘못이야

188 Oops. My mistake

아이고, 내 실수

189 I made a mistake

내가 실수했어

190 It was a simple mistake

단순한 실수였어

191 It was a big[huge] mistake

크나큰 실수였어

192 It is my fault

내 잘못이야

193 That's my fault

내 잘못이야

194 This is all[totally] my fault

모두 내 잘못야

195 I did it wrong

내가 잘못했어

196 It was careless of me to do so

내가 그렇게 한 건 부주의한 거였어

197 I went too far

너무 지나쳤어

198 I screwed up!

완전히 망했네!

199 I blew it

(기회 등을) 망쳤다, 날려버렸다

200 I guess I dropped the ball

큰 실수를 한 것 같아

201 I was way off (base)

내가 완전히 잘못 짚었네, 내 생각[행동]이 틀렸네

11 잘못해놓고 스스로 후회와 변명을 해보기

202 I shouldn't have done that

그러지 말았어야 했는데

203 # I shouldn't have said that

그렇게 말하는 게 아니었는데

204 # I should have asked him

걔한테 물어봤어야 하는데

205 # I feel so guilty

정말 미안해 죽겠어

206 # How silly[clumsy; stupid] of me!

내가 참 멍청하기도 하지!

207 # I regret doing that

그렇게 안하는 건데

208 # I wish I was dead

(잘못을 저지르고 미안해서) 미안해 죽겠어

209 # I wish it had never happened

그러지 않았더라면 좋았을텐데

210 # Please don't be offended

기분 상하지마

211
I was too nervous
내가 너무 긴장했었어

212
I didn't mean any harm
해를 끼칠려고 한 건 아니야

213
I didn't mean to cause you any trouble
너를 곤란케 하려는 건 아니었어

214
I was only trying to be funny
난 단지 웃자고 한거였는데

215
I didn't do it on purpose
일부러 그런 건 아니야

216
I did it just for kicks
그냥 재미삼아 해본 건데

217
No damage
손해본 건 없어

218
No harm (done)
잘못된거 없어

219 What's the harm?

손해볼게 뭐야?

12 다시는 그러지 않겠다고 다짐하기

220 I won't let it happen again

다신 그런 일 없을거야

221 I'll see it doesn't happen again

다신 그러지 않도록 조심할게요

222 I'll try to be more careful

더 조심하도록 노력할게

223 It won't happen again

이런 일 다시는 없을거야

224 It'll never happen again

다시는 이런 일 없을거야

225 (I swear) I won't do it again, I promise

다신 안 그러겠다고 맹세할게, 믿어줘

226

I take the blame

내가 책임질게

227

I have no excuses

변명의 여지가 없어

228

I want to try to make it up to you

내가 다 보상해줄게

229

I[We] will make it up to you

내[우리]가 다 보상할게

230

I'll try to make it up to you

보상하도록 할게

상황별 영어
대표문장

COMMON
SENTENCES
IN SITUATION
ENGLISH

05 위로

13 그럴 수도 있다고, 그나마 다행이라고 위로하기

231
That's (just) the way it is[goes]
다 그런 거지 뭐, 어쩔 수 없는 일이야

232
That's the way the cookie crumbles
사는 게 다 그런거지

233
That's the way the ball bounces
사는 게 다 그런거야

234
That's life
사는 게 그렇지

235
Such is life!
그런 게 인생이야!

236
That happens[happened]
그럴 수도 있지, 그런 일도 있기 마련이지

237
It happens
그럴 수도 있지 뭐

238 It happens to everybody[lots of people]

누구에게나 그럴 수 있어

239 Those[These] things happen

그런 일도 생기기 마련이야

240 Shit happens

(살다보면) 재수없는 일도 생기는 법이야

241 It could happen

그럴 수도 있겠지

242 It could happen to anyone

누구나 그럴 수 있어

243 I don't blame you

그럴 만도 해, 네가 어쩔 수 없었잖아

244 Don't blame yourself

너무 자책하지마

245 It's not your fault

네 잘못이 아니야

246 Everyone makes mistakes now and then

누구나 때때로 실수하는거야

247 It's a common mistake

그건 누구나 하는 실수인데

248 You have to expect a lot of ups and downs

좋을 때도 있고 안 좋을 때도 있는거야

249 It could[might] have been worse

그나마 다행이야

250 Win a few, lose a few

얻는 게 있으면 잃는 것도 있어

251 That was a close call

하마터면 큰일날 뻔했네. 위험천만이었어

14 별일아니니 걱정하지 말라고 위로하기

252 Don't worry

걱정마, 미안해할 것 없어

Don't worry about it

걱정마, 잘 될거야

Not to worry

걱정 안해도 돼

You don't have to worry

걱정하지마

There's nothing to worry about

걱정할 것 하나도 없어

There's no need to worry about it

걱정할 필요없어

That's all right

괜찮아

It's all right

괜찮아

It's[That's] okay

괜찮아

261 **No problem**

문제 없어

262 **Never mind**

신경쓰지마, 맘에 두지마

263 **That's[It's] no big deal**

별거 아냐

264 **No big deal**

별거 아냐

265 **What's the big deal?**

별거 아니네?, 무슨 큰 일이라도 있는거야?

266 **It was nothing**

별거 아닌데

267 **This is nothing**

별거 아니야

268 **Don't take it too seriously**

너무 심각하게 받아들이지마

269 Don't be sorry

미안해 하지마

270 You don't have to say you're sorry

미안해 할 필요없어

271 Don't sweat it!

(별일 아니니) 걱정하지 마라!

15 잊으라고 위로하기

272 Let it go

그냥 잊어버려, 그냥 놔둬

273 Would you let it go?

잊어버려요

274 Forget (about) it!

잊어버려!, 됐어!

275 Don't give it a second thought

걱정하지마

276 Don't give it another thought

잊어버려

277 Don't think about it anymore

더 이상 그것에 대해 생각하지마

278 Don't be so hard on yourself

너무 자책하지마

279 Don't let it bother you

너무 신경 쓰지매!

280 Don't let A get you down

A 때문에 괴로워하지마

281 Don't feel so bad about it

너무 속상해하지마

282 You must be very upset (about~)

(…에 대해서) 정말 화나겠어

283 You must be so upset

정말 화나겠구만

284 **Stop torturing yourself**

자학하지마

285 **Stop beating yourself up!**

그만 자책해라!

286 **Let's let bygones be bygones**

지나간 일은 잊자고

287 **It's no use crying over split milk**

엎지른 물을 다시 담을 수 없어

16 안됐다고 위로하기

288 **I'm sorry to hear that**

안됐네

289 **I'm sorry about that**

안됐어

290 **That's too bad**

저런, 안됐네, 이를 어쩌나

291

What a pity!

그것 참 안됐구나!

292

That's a pity!

참 안됐네!

293

What a shame!

안됐구나!

294

I know just how you feel

어떤 심정인지 알겠어

295

I know the feeling

그 심정 내 알지

296

That hurts

그거 안됐네, 마음이 아프겠구나

297

You poor thing

안됐구나

298

Oh, poor thing!

가엾은 거!

299

Ah, poor Jim!

아, 가엾은 짐!

300

It must be tough for you

참 어려웠겠구나

301

Tough luck

참 운도 없네

302

That's unfortunate

운이 없구만

303

How awful

참 안됐다

304

My heart goes out to you

진심으로 위로의 마음을 전합니다

305

You have all my sympathy

진심으로 유감의 말씀을 드립니다

306

I really sympathize with you

진심으로 위로의 말을 전합니다

COMMON
SENTENCES
IN SITUATION
ENGLISH

17 다 잘 될거라고 위로하기

307

Everything's going to be all right

다 잘 될거야

308

Everything will be fine

모든게 잘 될거야

309

She's going to be all right

걘 괜찮을거야

310

It's going to be all right

그건 괜찮을거야

311

It's going to be okay

잘 될거야, 괜찮을거야

312

Things will work out all right

잘 해결될거야

313

It's going to get better

더 잘 될거야

314 You're going to be great

넌 잘 될거다

315 It's all for the best

앞으로 나아질거야

316 You never know

그야 모르잖아, 그야 알 수 없지

You never know 주어+동사 …일지 누가 알아

317 You can never tell!

단정할 순 없지!

318 Your time will come

좋은 때가 올거야

Chapter

12

충고 · 불만

01 충고

1 진정하고 좀 쉬라고 충고하기

001

Take it easy

좀 쉬어가면서 해, 진정해, 잘 지내

002

Calm down

진정해

003

Calm down and think carefully

진정하고 잘 생각해봐

004

Cool down[off]

진정해

004

Be[Keep] cool

진정해라

005

Cool it

진정해, 침착해

007

Don't get[be] mad!

열받지 말라고!

008 # Don't get worked up

흥분하지마

009 # Don't get so uptight

그렇게 화내지말고

010 # Don't be upset!

화내지 말고!

011 # Go get some rest

가서 좀 쉬어

012 # Just relax!

긴장풀고 천천히 해!

2 상대방에게 조심하라고 주의를 줄 때

013 # Watch out

조심해

014 # Watch out for him!

걔 조심해!

015 Watch it!

조심해

016 Watch your step!

조심해!

Watch your step은 넘어지지 않도록 조심하라는 의미 뿐만 아니라 상대방에게 말이나 행동거지를 조심하라고 할 때도 쓰인다. 또한 Watch your back은 뒤(배신 등)를 조심하라는 표현.

017 Look out!

조심해!, 정신 차리라고!

018 (You) Be careful!

조심해!

019 Be careful of him

걔를 조심해

020 Heads up!

위험하니까 잘 보라구!

021 Behind you!

조심해!

3 급히 서두르지 말고 천천히하라고 충고하기

022
Easy does it
천천히 해, 조심조심, 진정해

023
Easy, easy, easy!
천천히!, 조심조심!

024
Take your time
천천히 해

025
Hold your horses
서두르지마, 진정해

026
What's the[your] rush?
왜 이리 급해?

027
What's the hurry?
왜 그렇게 서둘러?

028
There's[I'm] no hurry
서두를 것 없어, 급할 것 없어

029 There's no need to rush

서두를 필요없어

030 You don't need to hurry

서두르지 않아도 돼

031 No rush[hurry]

급할 거 없어

032 Slow down

천천히 해

033 Haste makes waste

서두르면 일을 망친다

034 We still have a long way to go

아직 가야할 길이 많아

035 Hurry up!

서둘러!

036 Step on it!

빨리 해, (자동차 엑셀레이터를) 더 밟아

037

I haven't got all day

여기서 이럴 시간 없어, 빨리 서둘러

038

Don't push (me)!

몰아 붙이지마!, 독촉하지마!

039

Get a move on it!

서둘러!

040

I'd better get a move on it

빨리 서둘러야겠어

041

Come on!

어서!, 그러지마!, 제발!, 자 덤벼!

4 철없는 친구에게 정신차리라고 따끔하게 말하기

042

Get a life!

정신차려!

043

Get real!

정신 좀 차리라구!

044

Don't even think about it

꿈도 꾸지마, 절대 안되니까 헛된 생각하지마

045

Don't you dare do that!

그럴 꿈도 꾸지매!

046

Act your age!

나이값 좀 해!

047

You have to grow up

철 좀 들어라

048

You can't have everything

너무 욕심내지마

049

Real life isn't that easy

사는 게 그렇게 쉽지는 않아

050

You wish!

행여나!

051

In your dreams!

꿈 깨셔!

052

Dream on!

꿈 한번 야무지네!

053

Stop goofing off!

그만 좀 빈둥거려라!

5 행동에 앞서 신중히 꼼꼼히 생각해보라고 말하기

054

Think twice before you do it

실행하기에 앞서 한번 더 생각해봐

055

Think it over carefully before you decide

결정에 앞서 신중히 생각해봐

056

You shouldn't be so quick to judge!

그렇게 섣불리 판단해선 안돼!

057

You can't be too careful

아무리 조심해도 지나치지 않아

058

(It's) Better safe than sorry

뒤늦게 후회하느니 조심해야지

059 Don't jump to conclusions!

섣부르게 판단하지마!

060 Let's not jump the gun

경솔하게 속단하지마

061 Don't count your chickens before they're hatched

김치국부터 마시지마

062 Don't judge a book by its cover

겉만 보고 속을 판단하지마

063 Never judge something by its looks

뭐든 외양만 갖고 판단하면 안돼

064 Don't fall for it

(속아) 넘어가지 마, 사랑에 빠지면 안돼

065 Don't trust it

믿지마

066 Don't be so impatient

너무 조급해하지마

067

He's better than you think

걔는 네가 생각하는거 이상야

068

You'll be sorry

넌 후회하게 될거야

069

You'll regret it

넌 후회하게 될거야

070

You (just) wait and see

두고보라고

071

We'll see

좀 보자고, 두고 봐야지

072

You'll see

곧 알게 될거야, 두고 보면 알아

073

Let's wait and see how things go

일이 어떻게 돼가는지 지켜보자

6 말을 신중히 가려서 하라고 충고할 때

074 Watch your tongue!

말 조심해!

075 Watch your language[mouth]

말 조심해

076 Hold your tongue!

제발 그 입 좀 다물어!

077 Bite your tongue

입 조심해, 말이 씨가 되는 수가 있어

078 You've got a big mouth

너 참 입이 싸구나

079 Big mouth!

입 한번 엄청 싸네!

080 Shut up!

닥쳐!

081 Shut your face!

입다물어!

082 **You talk too much**

말이 너무 많네

---

7 시간낭비하지 말라고 충고하기

083 **Don't waste your time**

시간 낭비하지마, 시간낭비야

084 **Don't waste my time**

남의 귀한 시간 축내지마, 괜히 시간낭비 시키지 말라고

085 **You're (just) wasting my time**

시간낭비야, 내 시간 낭비마

086 **It's a waste of time**

시간낭비야

087 **What a waste of time and money!**

시간과 돈 낭비야!

088 **I don't like wasting my time**

시간낭비하고 싶지 않아

089 **It isn't worth it**

그럴만한 가치가 없어, 그렇게 중요한 것도 아닌데

090 **It isn't worth the trouble**

괜히 번거롭기만 할거야

8 제대로 하라고 주의를 줄 때

091 **Do it right**

제대로 해

092 **Let's just do it right**

제대로나 하자

093 **We can do it right!**

우린 제대로 잘 할 수 있어!

094 **Use your head!**

머리를 좀 쓰라구!, 생각이라는 걸 좀 해라!

095 **Where's your head at?**

머리는 어디다 둔거야?

096

You heard me

명심해

097

You'll get the hang[knack] of it

금방 손에 익을거야, 요령이 금방 붙을거야

098

(There's) Nothing to it

아주 쉬워, 해보면 아무것도 아냐

099

You have to get used to it

적응해야지

100

I'm getting used to it

난 적응하고 있어

101

Don't leave things half done

일을 하다 말면 안돼

102

You should finish what you start

시작한 건 끝내야지

9 다시 그러지말라고 경고하기

103

Don't let it happen again

다신 그러지마

104

Please be sure it doesn't happen again

다신 그러지 않도록 해

105

Not again!

어휴 또야, 어떻게 또 그럴 수 있어!

106

Please don't do that

제발 그러지마

107

Don't do that anymore

더는 그러지마

108

Don't ever do that again

두번 다시 그러지마

109

You can't do that!

그러면 안되지!

110

We can't do that

우리가 그러면 안되지

111 Here we go again

또 시작이군

112 There you go again

또 시작이군

113 Haven't you learned your lesson yet?

아직 따끔한 맛을 못봤어?

114 Don't make such stupid mistakes again!

다신 그런 어리석은 실수하지마라!

🔟 상대방에게 뭔가를 하지 말라고 충고할 때

115 You shouldn't say things like that

그렇게 말하면 안되지

You shouldn't + 동사~ …해서는 안돼

116 You must not hit your children

때론. 얘들을 치면 안돼지

You must not + 동사~ …해서는 안돼

117 You'd better not go outside. It's too cold

나가지 마. 밖은 너무 추워

You'd better not + 동사~ …하지 않는 게 좋아

118 You're not supposed to do that

그러면 안되는데

You're not supposed to + 동사~ 너는 …해서는 안돼

119 I'm not supposed to be here

난 여기 있으면 안되는데

120 You don't want to use that computer

그 컴퓨터는 사용하지 않는 게 좋아

You don't want to + 동사~ …하지 마라

121 You don't have to walk me home

집까지 안 데려다 줘도 되는데

You don't have to + 동사~ …안해도 돼

122 You should know better than to tell him a secret

너 그 사람한테 비밀을 말하면 안되는 줄은 알았을 것 아냐

You should know better than~ …하지 않을 정도는 돼야지

123 Don't touch me

만지지마

Don't + 동사 …하지 마라

124 Don't cut in line

끼어들지마

125 Don't be selfish

이기적이지 마라

Don't be + 형용사 …하지 마라

126 Don't be jealous

질투하지 마라

127 If I were you, I wouldn't let him know until tomorrow

내가 너라면, 내일이나 걔한테 말할텐데

If I were you, I wouldn't + 동사~ 너라면 난 …하지 않을 텐데

128 I wouldn't if I were you

내가 너라면 그렇게 하지 않겠어

11 상대방에게 뭔가를 하라고 충고할 때

129 Do it yourself

스스로 해라

130 Do as[what] I said!

내가 말한대로 해!

131 Do what I told you to do!

내가 지시한 대로 하라고!

132 Be good to others

다른 사람들에게 잘 대해

Be+형용사 …해라

133 Be strong!

건강하라고!

134 Be a good boy

착한 애가 돼라

Be+명사 …가 돼라

135 Be a man!

남자답게 행동해라!

136 You should do it this way

넌 이런 식으로 그걸 해야 돼

137 This is the way you should do it

이런 방식으로 그걸 해야 돼

138 This is the first thing to do

가장 먼저 해야 되는 건 이거야

139 You should do this first

이걸 먼저 해야 돼

140

Let me give you a piece of advice

내가 네게 충고 좀 할게

141

I'm telling you this from experience

내 경험상으로 말하는 건데

142

What you need is a little more effort

조금만 더 노력하면 돼

143

Better than nothing

아무 것도 안 하는 것보단 낫지

144

It's your responsibility

너의 책임야

145

It's your duty

너의 의무야

146

That's the name of the game

그게 가장 중요한거야

147

That's the most important thing

그게 가장 중요한거야

12 상대방의 말이나 행동을 잠시 제지하고 싶을 때

148 **Wait a minute, please!**

잠깐만요!

149 **Just[wait] a moment**

잠깐만

150 **Hold on (a second)!**

잠깐!

151 **Hold it!**

잠깐, 그대로 있어!

152 **Stop that[it]!**

그만해!

153 **Just drop it!**

당장 그만둬!

154 **Don't move!**

움직이지마!

155 Don't make a move!

움직이지마!

156 Freeze!

꼼짝마!

157 Stop saying that!

닥치라고!, 그만 좀 얘기해!

158 Cut it out!

그만둬!, 닥쳐!

159 Knock it off

조용히 해

160 Come off it!

집어쳐!, 건방떨지마!

161 Cut the crap

바보 같은 소리마, 쓸데 없는 이야기 좀 그만둬

162 Listen to yourself

멍청한 소리 그만해

13 상대방에게 실망이나 불만이 있을 때

163 Don't disappoint me

실망시키지마

164 This is disappointing

실망스럽구만

165 What a disappointment!

참 실망스럽네!

166 Don't let me down

기대를 저버리지 마

167 You let me down

너한테 실망했어

168 I'm ashamed of you

부끄러운 일이야, 부끄러워 혼났어

169 You should be ashamed (of yourself)

창피한 줄 알아

170 **Aren't you ashamed of yourself?**

창피한 줄도 몰라?

171 **Shame on you**

부끄러운 줄 알아야지, 창피한 일이야

172 **For shame**

창피한 일이야

173 **I was frustrated with you**

너 때문에 맥이 풀렸어

174 **I'm bummed out**

실망이야

175 **I don't like it**

마음에 안들어

176 **I'm not happy with it**

만족못해, 마음에 안들어

177 **Do you have a problem with me?**

나한테 뭐 불만있는 거야?

178 Does anybody have a problem with that?

누구 문제 있는 사람 있어?

179 Do you have a problem with that?

그게 뭐 문제있어?

02 불만

14 정도를 넘어서는 상대방에게 짜증내기

180 That's (just) too much!

해도 해도 너무해, 그럴 필요는 없는데!

181 That's asking too much

너무 많이 요구하는 구만

182 You're going too far

너무하는군

183 You go too far

너 오바야

184 You have gone too far

네가 너무했어, 심했다

185 What do you want from me?

나보고 어쩌라는거야?

186 He went overboard

그 사람이 좀 너무했어

187 Don't go overboard

과식[과음]하지마

188 How can you say that?

어떻게 그렇게 말할 수 있나?

189 How could you say such a thing?

네가 어떻게 그런 말을 할 수 있니?

190 How could you not tell us?

어떻게 우리에게 말하지 않을 수 있지?

191 How could you do that?

어쩌면 그럴 수가 있어?

192 How could you do this to me[us]?

내[우리]한테 어떻게 이럴 수 있니?

193 How dare you insult me!

감히 날 모욕하다니!

How dare you + 동사~ ? 어떻게 …할 수가 있어?

15 상대방에게 맘대로 하라고 말하기

194 **You wouldn't dare (to do something)!**

어쩜 감히 이럴 수가!

195 **You're pushing your luck**

운을 과신하는 구만, 화를 부르는 구만

196 **Have[Do] it your way**

네 맘대로 해, 좋을 대로 해

197 **He gets his way**

걘 제멋대로야

198 **Suit yourself!**

네 멋대로 해!, 맘대로 해!

199 **Do what you want**

원하는 대로 해

200 **Do whatever you want**

뭐든 원하는 대로 해

201 Do as you please

맘대로 해

202 Do as you like

좋을 대로 해

03 싸움

16 날 놀리지 말라고 경고하기

203 # What do you take me for?

날 뭘로 보는거야?

204 # Who do you think you're talking to?

너 나한테 그렇게 말하면 재미없어

205 # Who do you think you're kidding?

설마 나더러 그 말을 믿으라는 건 아니지

206 # You're pulling my leg

나 놀리는거지, 농담이지

207 # Are you pulling my leg?

나 놀리는거니?

208 # Don't pull my leg

놀리지마

209 # Do I look like I was born yesterday?

내가 그렇게 어리숙해보여?

210 I wasn't born yesterday!

누굴 햇병아리로 보내!

211 How dumb do you think I am?

내가 바본 줄 아니?, 누굴 바보로 아는 거니?

212 Why are you picking on me?

왜 날 괴롭히는거야?

213 I'm not stupid

난 바보가 아냐

214 Are you trying to make a fool of me?

나를 놀리려고 하는거야?

215 You're telling me that you can't finish it?

그걸 끝내지 못한다는거야?

You're telling me that 주어+동사~? …라고 말하는 거야? 말투나 상황에 따라 상대방의 말을
확인하거나 혹은 시비를 걸 때 사용한다.

216 Stop kidding[joking]

농담하지마

217 Don't make fun of me!

나 놀리지마

218 You're making fun of me?

너 지금 나 놀리냐?

220 Don't tease me!

놀리지마!

221 You're teasing me

나 놀리는거지

17 상대방보고 꺼지라고 소리치기

221 Get out of here!

꺼져!, 웃기지마!

222 Get out of my face!

내 눈 앞에서 안보이게 사라져!

223 Get out of my way

비켜라, 방해하지 마라

224 Go away!

꺼져!

225 **Get lost!**

(그만 좀 괴롭히고) 꺼져!

226 **(You) Back off!**

비키시지!

227 **You stay out of it!**

좀 비켜라!

228 **Keep[Stay] out of my way**

가로 막지 좀 마

229 **Stay away from me!**

꺼져!

230 **(You) Just watch!**

넌 보고만 있어!

231 **Don't mess with me**

나 건드리지마

232 **I don't want to get in the way**

방해되고 싶지 않아

18 예의없는 행동을 하는 상대방을 야단치기

233

Behave yourself

버릇없이 굴면 안돼(아이들에게), 점잖게 행동해

234

Where are your manners?

매너가 그게 뭐야, 매너가 없구나

235

Remember your manners

버릇없이 굴지 말구, 예의를 지켜야지

236

Mind your manners!

방정맞게 굴지마!

237

Be sure to mind your manners!

예의바르게 굴도록 해!

238

Mind your P's and Q's!

품행[말]을 조심해라

239

Don't be rude!

무례하게 굴지마!

240 Watch your step

말(혹은 행동거지) 조심해

241 Your behavior is out of place

네 행동은 무례한 짓이야

242 Be on your best behavior

점잖게 행동해라

243 You have a bad attitude

너 태도가 안 좋구나

244 I don't like your attitude

너 태도가 맘에 안 들어

245 Manners count, even between close friends

친할수록 예의를 지켜야지

246 Use good etiquette

예의바르게 행동해

19 이상한 행동을 하는 상대방에게 미쳤냐고 말하기

250 **You crazy?**

너 미쳤어?

251 **Are you insane[nuts]?**

너 돌았니?

252 **You're driving me crazy**

너 때문에 미치겠다

253 **You've driving me up the wall**

너 때문에 미치겠다

251 **What do you think you're doing?**

이게 무슨 짓이야, 너 정신 나갔어?

252 **Are you out of your mind?**

너 제 정신이야?

253 **You're out of your mind!**

너 미쳤구만!

254 **He's out to lunch**

걔 요즘 얼이 빠져있어

255 **You are not yourself**

제정신이 아니네

256 **I'm not myself**

나 지금 제 정신이 아냐

257 **Is he all there?**

걔 미쳤어?

258 **He's not all there**

잰 정신나갔나봐

259 **There's nobody home!**

정신 어디다 두고 있는거야!

260 **The lights are on but nobody's home**

어쩜 그렇게 맹하고 느려터졌니

261 **Anybody home?**

집에 아무도 없어요?, 정신있니 없니?

262 I'm losing my mind
내가 제 정신이 아니야

263 You seem spaced out
너 정신이 나간 것 같구나

20 상대방 말이 말도 안된다고 못믿겠다고 받아치기

264 It doesn't make any sense
무슨 소리야, 말도 안돼

265 It makes no sense
그건 말도 안돼

266 Does that make any sense?
그게 말이 돼?

267 Don't be ridiculous
바보같이 굴지 마

268 Don't be silly[foolish]
바보같이 굴지마

269 This is ridiculous

이건 말도 안돼

270 This is crazy[nuts]

이건 말도 안되는 짓이야, 말도 안돼

271 Don't make me laugh!

웃기지 좀 매, 웃음 밖에 안 나온다!

272 Don't lie to me

거짓말하지마

273 Don't tell me lies

거짓말하지마

274 That's a lie!

거짓말야!

275 Liar!

거짓말쟁이!

276 Don't say stupid things

바보 같은 말 하지마

277 Don't play dumb!

순진한 척하지마!

278 Don't give me that!

그런 말 마!, 정말 시치미떼기야!

21 변명하는 상대방에게 일침하기

279 That's no excuse

그건 변명거리가 안돼

280 No more excuses!

변명은 그만해!

281 Don't make any excuses!

변명 좀 그만해!

282 I've heard enough of your excuses

네 변명은 이젠 지겨워

283 That's not a good excuse

그럴 듯한 변명도 아니네

284 I don't want to hear any excuses

어떤 변명도 듣고 싶지 않아

285 That doesn't excuse your behavior

그렇다고 너의 행동을 용인할 수가 없어

286 That hardly explains your actions

그건 너의 행동에 대한 변명이 안돼

287 Tell me another

거짓말마, 말이 되는 소리를 해라

288 Spare me!

집어치워!, 그만둬!

289 No ifs, ands or buts!

군말 말고 시키는 대로 해!

290 Now what?

그래서 뭐?

22 간섭하는 상대방에게 상관하지 말라고 하기

291 **It's none of your business**

남의 일에 신경쓰지마, 참견마

292 **Mind your own business!**

상관 말라구!

293 **I'll thank you to mind your own business**

신경꺼주면 고맙겠어

294 **That's really my business**

그건 내일이니 신경꺼

295 **Keep[Get] your nose out of my business**

내 일에 참견마

296 **Stay out of this!**

상관매, 참견매!

Stay out of this!는 개인적인 문제이니까 "참견하지 마라"라는 의미이며 Stay away (from me)는 "내 면전에서 꺼지라"라고 말하는 경고성 문구이다.

297 **Don't get involved**

상관마

Chapter 12

461

298 Who asked you?

누가 너한테 물었어?

299 Who cares what you think?

누가 너한테 물어봤어?, 맘대로 생각해라

300 Butt out!

참견말고 꺼져!, 가서 네 일이나 잘해!

301 It's not your concern

상관마

302 It's personal

개인적인거야

23 내가 일을 그르치거나 상대방에게 당했을 경우

303 You caught me

들켰다

304 He caught me smoking

담배피우다 그 사람한테 들켰어

305

You screwed me!

날 속였군!

306

You did a number on me

내가 당했구만

307

I'm so busted

딱 걸렸어

308

Gotcha!

잡았다!, 속았지!, 당했지!, 알았어!

309

I'm fucking with you

널 놀리는거야

310

She gave it to me

나 걔한테 혼쭐이 났어

24 안 좋은 일을 당한 상대방에 당해싸다고 질책하기

311

You asked for it

자업자득이지, 네가 자초한 일이잖아, 그런 일을 당해도 싸다

Chapter **12**

312 You'll pay for that!

당해도 싸다!, 꼴 좋군!

313 You had it coming!

네가 자초한거야!

314 (It) Serves you right!

넌 그런 일 당해도 싸, 꼴 좋다!

315 That'll teach her!

그래도 싸지, 당연한 대가야

316 Well, that'll teach you a lesson

그래, 이제 좀 정신차리겠지

317 You'll never get away with it

넌 그걸 피할 수 없어

318 Well, you got what you deserved

당해 싸다

319 You've brought this on yourself

네가 초래한거야

320 There's no reason to complain

당연한 결과지

25 나한테 못되게구는 상대방에게 경고하기

321 You can't do this to me

나한테 이러면 안되지, 이러지마

322 Why are you doing this to me?

내게 왜 이러는거야?

323 What have you done to me?

내게 무슨 짓을 한거야?

324 Don't tell me what to do!

나에게 이래라 저래라 하지마!

325 Don't call me names!

욕하지마!

326 Don't blame me

나한테 뭐라고 하지마

327 Don't insult me

날 모욕하지마

328 Don't say it's my fault

내 잘못이라고 하지마

329 I didn't do anything wrong!

난 잘못한 것 하나도 없어!

330 You're to blame

네가 잘못이다

331 You can't talk to me like that

내게 그렇게 말하면 안돼

332 Don't look at me like that

그런 식으로 날 보지마

333 Don't talk back to me!

내게 말대꾸하지마!

334 Take it back

취소해

335 # I don't want to cause problems

문제 일으키고 싶지 않아

336 # Why are you trying to make me feel bad?

왜 날 기분 나쁘게 만드는거야?

26 **한심한 상대방을 대놓고 무시하기**

337 # You don't know the first thing about it

아무것도 모르면서, 쥐뿔도 모르면서

338 # You don't know the half of it

별로 알지도 못하면서

339 # You have no idea

넌 모를거야

340 # You have no idea what this means to me!

이게 내게 얼마나 중요한 건지 넌 몰라!

341 # You have no idea how much I need this

이게 내게 얼마나 필요한지 넌 몰라

342 You have no idea how much this hurts

이게 얼마나 아픈지 넌 모를거야

343 What do you know about love?

네가 사랑이 뭔지 알기나 해?

What do you know about + 명사? …에 대해 네가 뭘 알아?

344 You never learn

넌 구제불능이야

27 잘난 척하는 상대방 한번에 기죽이기

345 Who do you think you are?

네가 도대체 뭐가 그리도 잘났는데?

346 Don't be a smart-ass

건방지게 굴지마

347 Don't be smart with me!

잘난체 하지마!

348 You think you're so smart[big]

네가 그렇게 똑똑한 줄 알아

349 You are nothing special

당신 대단한거 없어

350 Look who's talking

사돈 남말하네

351 You're one to talk

사돈 남 말하시네

352 Very funny!

그래 우습기도 하겠다!

353 Take your own advice

너나 잘해

354 Don't be bossy

뻐기지마

28 밥맛인 상대방과 한판뜨기

355 Bring it on!

한번 덤벼봐!, 어디 한번 해보자구!

COMMON
SENTENCES
IN SITUATION
ENGLISH

356 Gang up on me!

다 덤벼봐!

357 Bite me

배 째라!, 어쩌라구!

주로 10대들이 쓰는 무례한 표현으로 성인들 사이에서는 농담조로 쓰인다.

358 Make my day!

할테면 해봐라!

359 Go ahead, make my day!

덤벼봐, 한번 해보자구!

360 He's a dead man

쟨 이제 죽었다

361 It's your funeral

그 날로 넌 끝이야

362 So sue me

그럼 고소해 봐

363 We've got to get even

되갚아 줘야 돼

364 I want to get even with him
앙갚음 하겠어

365 I lost my temper
내가 열받았어

366 I've run out of patience
더 이상 못참아

367 Stop fighting!
그만 싸워!

368 Did you make up?
화해했니?

369 Let's make up
화해하자

370 Can't you patch things up?
화해가 안돼?

Common Sentences
in Situation English

Chapter

13

기쁨 · 슬픔

상황별 영어
대표문장

COMMON
SENTENCES
IN SITUATION
ENGLISH

01 기쁨

1 내가 기쁠 때 말하는 여러가지 방법들

001 I'm so happy

정말 기뻐

002 I'm so excited[thrilled]

정말 신나[짜릿해]

003 I'm glad to hear that

그것 참 잘됐다, 좋은 소식이라 기쁘다

004 That's great to hear

참 잘됐어

005 I'm glad you like it

네가 좋다니 기뻐

I'm glad that 주어+동사 …해서 너무 기뻐

006 I feel great[good]

기분 아주 좋아

007 I feel terrific

기분 끝내줘

008

I feel a lot better now

기분이 좀 나아져

009

You made me happy

너 때문에 행복해

010

It makes me feel better

그 때문에 기분이 좋아졌어

011

That makes me feel so good

그게 기분을 좋게 해줘

012

I'm in a good mood today

오늘 기분이 좋아

013

It was really fun

정말 재밌었어

014

I had a good time

즐거웠어

015

I got lucky

운이 좋았어

016 I was just lucky

그냥 운이 좋았어

017 It was just luck

운이 좋았던거야

018 I've never been this happy

이처럼 행복한 적이 없어

019 I couldn't be happier

정말이지 아주 행복해

020 This is the happiest moment in my life

내 인생에서 가장 행복한 순간야

021 I'm relieved to hear that

그 이야기를 들으니 맘이 놓여

022 What a relief!

참 다행이야!

02 슬픔

2 기분 나쁘고 슬프고 외로울 때

023

I'm not in the mood

그럴 기분이 아냐

024

I'm in a bad mood

기분이 안좋아

025

I'm under the weather

몸이 찌뿌둥해

026

I'm feeling a little sick

몸상태가 좀 안좋네

027

I don't feel like doing anything

아무 것도 하기 싫어

028

I feel sad

슬퍼

029

I'm sad[unhappy]

슬퍼[행복하지 않아]

030 I'm depressed

지쳤어

031 It's really frustrating

정말 맥빠지게 해

embarrass, frustrate, depress, interest 등은 모두 타동사로 ~ing을 붙여 embarrassing 하게 되면 「…을 당황케하는」이라는 의미이고 반면 embarrassed하면 「…에 의해 당황한」이라 는 뜻이 된다.

032 It's depressing

지치게 해

033 I've got the blues today

오늘 울적해

034 He looks gloomy today

걔 오늘 우울해보여

035 I miss you

그립다

036 That's just my luck

내가 그렇지 뭐

037   Tough break!
재수 옴 붙었군!

038   I feel so used
기분 참 더럽네

상황별 영어
대표문장

COMMON
SENTENCES
IN SITUATION
ENGLISH

03 곤란·당황

3 난처하고 곤란한 상황에서

039
I don't know what to do
어떻게 해야 할지 모르겠어

040
I don't know what to say
뭐라 해야할 지 모르겠어

041
I don't know what else to do
달리 어떻게 해야 할 지 모르겠어

042
What should I do?
어떻게 해야 하지?

043
What am I supposed to do?
내가 어떻게 해야 되지?

044
What am I going to do?
어떻게 하지?

045
What am I going to say?
뭐라고 말하지?

046 I'm so humiliated
쪽 팔려, 창피해 죽겠어

047 This is a slap in the face
창피해서 원, 치욕스러워라

048 That's so embarrassing!
정말 황당하다!

049 How embarrassing!
정말 당혹해라!

050 You embarrass me
너 때문에 창피하다

051 I'm so embarrassed
당황했어

052 I got screwed
망신 당했어, 수모를 당했어

053 We're in trouble
곤란한 상황야

054 I'm ashamed of myself

창피해

055 I'm ashamed that I did that

내가 한 일로 창피해

056 It's a big problem

문제가 커

057 It's a really serious problem

정말 곤란한 문제야

058 It's a pain in the neck[ass]

골칫거리야

059 That's the hard part

그게 어려운 부분야

114 오늘일진

4 오늘 하루가 좋거나 안좋을 때

060
This is not my day
정말 일진 안좋네

061
This is not your[his] day
오늘은 네가[걔가] 되는 게 없는 날이다

062
Today wasn't my day
오늘 정말 일진 안좋았어

063
Today is my lucky day
오늘 일진 좋네

064
What a lucky day!
정말 운 좋은 날이네!

065
This must be my lucky day!
오늘은 내가 운이 좋을거야!

066
It's your lucky day
너 재수 좋은 날이야

067 I had a bad day

진짜 재수없는 날이야

068 I'm having a really bad day

정말 오늘 안좋네

069 I had a rough day

힘든 하루였어

070 Rough day for you?

힘든 하루였지?

071 It has been a long day

힘든 하루였어

072 I'm not feeling up to par today

오늘은 좀 평소와 달라, 컨디션이 좀 안좋아

073 It hasn't been your day

되는 일이 아무 것도 없는 날이야

074 Boy, what a day!

야, 정말 짜증나는 날이야!

05 짜증

5 지겨워 못 참겠다고 짜증내기

075
That's enough!
이제 그만!, 됐어 그만해!

076
That's enough for now
이젠 됐어

077
I've had enough of you
이제 너한테 질렸어

078
I've had enough of it!
이제 지겨워 죽겠다!

079
Enough is enough!
이젠 충분해!

080
I'm sick of this
진절머리가 나

081
I'm fed up with it!
진절머리나!

082 It's boring

지루해, 따분해

083 I've had it[enough]!

지겹다!, 넌더리나!

084 I've had it with you guys

너희들한테 질려버렸다

have it with somebody[something] 「…라면 질렸다」라는 숙어.

085 I've had it up to here with you

너라면 이제 치가 떨려, 너한테 질려버렸어

086 I've had it up to here

아주 지긋지긋해

087 I can't take it anymore

더 이상 못 견디겠어요

088 I can't stand this

이건 못참겠어

089 I can't stand your friends

네 친구들은 정말 지겨워

090 I can't stand losing
지고는 못살아

091 That's the last straw
해도해도 너무 하는군, 더 이상 못참겠어

6 귀찮게 하지 말고 가만 좀 놔두라고 면박줄 때

092 Leave me alone
나 좀 내버려둬, 귀찮게 좀 하지마

093 Leave me in peace
나 좀 가만히 내버려둬

094 Give me a break
좀 봐줘요, 그만 좀 해라

095 Give it a rest!
그만 좀 하지 그래!

096 Stop bothering me
나 좀 가만히 놔둬

097 Don't bother me

귀찮게 하지 좀 마

098 Stop picking on me

못살게 굴지 좀 마

099 Please stop bugging me

나 좀 귀찮게 하지마

100 Stop pestering me

그만 좀 괴롭혀

101 Get your hands off of me!

내 몸에서 손떼!

102 Get off my back

귀찮게 굴지 말고 나 좀 내버려둬

103 Get off my case

귀찮게 하지 좀 마

104 Go easy on me

좀 봐줘

go easy on something하게 되면 「…을 적당히 하다」라는 의미의 표현으로 예로 Go easy on
the whisky하면 "위스키 좀 적당히 마셔"라는 뜻.

105 Have a heart

한번만 봐줘, 온정을 베풀라구

106 Don't be so hard on me

나한테 그렇게 심하게 하지마, 그렇게 빡빡하게 굴지마

107 Don't give me a hard time

나 힘들게 하지마

108 Cut me some slack

좀 봐줘요, 여유를 좀 줘, 너무 몰아세우지마

109 I can cut him some slack

걔를 좀 봐줄 수도 있지

7 짜증나 열받은 경우에

110 I'm pissed off!

열받아!, 진절머리나!

111 She made me mad

걔 때문에 화나

112 I'm mad[angry; upset]

화나, 열받아

113 He got worked up

걔 열 받았어, 걔 대단했어

114 You're a pain in the neck[ass]

너 참 성가시네

115 You're getting on my nerves

신경거슬리게 하네

116 You're bothering me

너 때문에 귀찮아

117 That burns me (up)!

정말 열받네!

118 It's really getting to me

진짜 짜증나게 하네

119 She really gets to me

걔때문에 열받아(= She really makes me mad)

120 This makes me sick
역겨워

121 That's disgusting
정떨어진다

122 That's gross
역겨워

123 It sucks!
밥맛이야!, 젠장할!

124 That[This] sucks!
빌어먹을!

125 You suck!
재수없어!

126 This vacation sucks
이번 휴가는 엉망진창이야

127 It stinks
젠장, 영 아니야!, 냄새가 지독해

128

That marriage stinks

저 결혼은 영 아니야

06 놀람·감탄

8 믿을 수 없는 일을 겪거나 충격받았을 때

129 I can't believe it!

설마!, 말도 안돼!, 그럴 리가!,이럴 수가!

130 I can't believe you did that

네가 그랬다는 게 믿기지 않아

131 I don't believe this!

이건 말도 안돼!

132 I don't believe it!

그럴 리가!

133 Unbelievable!

믿을 수가 없어!

134 Incredible!

믿기지 않아!

135 Awesome!

끝내주네!, 대단하네!

136 I'm surprised[shocked]

놀랐어[충격야]

137 What a surprise[shock]!

놀라워라!

138 You surprised[scared] me

너 때문에 놀랐어

139 Isn't it amazing?

대단하지 않아?, 정말 놀랍지 않아?

140 That's amazing!

거 대단하다!

141 Isn't that great?

대단하지 않니?

142 How about that!

거 근사한데!, 그거 좋은데!

143 Imagine that!

어 정말야?, 놀라워라!

144 How do you do that?

어쩜 그렇게 잘하니?, 어떻게 해낸거야?

145 What a coincidence!

이런 우연이!

146 What a small world!

세상 참 좁네!

147 It's a small world

세상 참 좁네요

148 You don't say!

설마!, 아무려면!, 정말!, 뻔한거 아냐!

149 Don't tell me!

설마!

150 I never heard of such a thing

말도 안돼

151 What do you know!

놀랍군!, 네가 뭘 안다고!

152 **Fancy that!**

설마, 도저히 믿기지 않는다!

153 **I'm speechless**

할말이 없어, 말이 안나와

154 **Would you believe he gave me a car?**

내게 차를 줬는데 놀랍지 않아?

Would you believe 주어+동사? …가 믿겨져?

155 **Would you believe it?**

그게 정말이야?

156 **It was the last thing I expected**

생각도 못했어

9 어떻게 이런 일이 있을 수 있나 탄식하기

157 **How could this[that] happen?**

어떻게 이럴 수가 있니?

158 **How can this be happening?**

어떻게 이런 일이 일어나는 거지?

159 How could this happen to me?!

나한테 어떻게 이런 일이 생긴단 말야?!

160 It never happened

이런 적 한번도 없었어

161 That never happened to me

이런 경험 처음이야

162 That has never happened before

난생 처음 겪는 일이야

163 Can you believe this is already happening?

벌써 이렇게 됐어?

164 I guess I just can't believe any of this is happening

이런 일이 생기다니 믿을 수가 없는걸

165 How is that possible?

어떻게 그럴 수가 있지?

166 That can't be good[smart]

그럴 리 없어, 안 좋을텐데

167 It can't be

이럴 수가

168 It can't be true

그럴 리가 없어

169 Something's wrong

뭔가 잘못된거야

170 That's (so) weird

거 (정말) 이상하네

171 This feels (very) weird

이상한 것 같아

172 That's funny

거참 이상하네, 거참 신기하다

Chapter

14

부탁 · 제안

상황별 영어
대표문장

COMMON
SENTENCES
IN SITUATION
ENGLISH

01 부탁

1 상대방에게 도움을 부탁할 때

001 ## Can[Would] you give me a hand?

좀 도와줄래?

002 ## Could[Would] you do me a favor?

부탁 좀 들어줄래요?

003 ## Can[May] I ask you a favor?

좀 도와 줄래요?

004 ## Can[May] I ask you something?

뭐 좀 부탁해도 돼?, 뭐 좀 물어봐도 돼?

005 ## I'd like to ask you something

뭐 좀 부탁할게[물어볼게]

006 ## Let me ask you something

뭐 좀 부탁할게[물어볼게]

007 ## Can you help me?

나 좀 도와줄래?

008
Would you please help me?
좀 도와줄래요?

009
I need to ask for your help
네 도움이 필요해

010
I need to ask you for some help
네게 도움 좀 청해야 겠어

011
Would you help me set up the computer?
컴퓨터를 설치하는 거 도와줄래요?

Would you help me + 동사[with+명사]? …하는 걸 좀 도와줄래요?

012
Would you lend me your phone?
전화기 좀 빌려줄테야?

Would you + 동사~? …해줄래요?

013
I'd like you to come to my party
파티에 왔으면 좋겠어

I'd like you to + 동사 네가 …을 해주었으면 좋겠어

014
I want you to be my friend again
다시 나랑 친구하자

I want you to + 동사 네가 …을 해줘

015 I'd appreciate it if you could bring an appetizer

전채요리를 가져다 주면 감사하겠어요

I'd appreciate it if you would + 동사~ …해주면 고맙겠어요

016 I'd be pleased if you could join us for dinner

저녁식사를 함께 했으면 좋겠네요

I would be pleased if you + 동사 …해주면 좋겠어요

017 Consider it done

그렇게 하지

018 No strings (attached)

아무런 조건없이

2 상대방에게 뭐 도와줄 게 없는지 먼저 물어보기

019 What can I do for you?

뭘 도와줄까?

020 Is there anything I can do for you?

뭐 도와줄 것 없어?

021 Do you want any help?

좀 도와줄까?

022 Need any help?

도와줘?

023 Do you need some help?

뭐 좀 도와줄까?

024 Can I give you a hand?

도와줄까?

025 Do you need a hand?

도와줄까?

026 If there's anything you need, don't hesitate to ask

필요한 거 있으면 바로 말해

027 If you need any help, just call

뭐 도움이 필요하면 전화해

028 If you need me, you know where I am

도움이 필요하면 바로 불러

029 You know where to find me

내 연락처는 알고 있지

030

Feel free to ask

뭐든 물어봐, 맘껏 물어봐

031

I'd be happy to help you

기꺼이 도와줄게요

032

I'd be glad to do it

기꺼이 그렇게 할게요

033

With pleasure

기꺼이

034

I'll do anything for you

뭐든지 해줄게

035

Anything for you

널 위해선 뭐든지

036

What are friends for?

친구 좋다는 게 뭐야?

037

Sure. What is it?

그래. 뭔대?

038 Sure. How can I help?

그래. 어떻게 도와줄까?

039 Sure, what can I do?

그래, 내가 어떻게 해줄까?

040 Have you had any problems?

뭐 문제있어?

041 Is there a problem?

문제가 있는거야?

042 What seems to be the problem?

문제가 뭐인 것 같아?

상황별 영어
대표문장

COMMON
SENTENCES
IN SITUATION
ENGLISH

02 허가

3 상대방에게 뭔가 해도 되냐고 허가받기

043

Is it okay to come in?

들어가도 돼?

044

Is it okay if I go out now?

지금 가도 돼?

Is it okay[all right] to[if]~ ~? …해도 괜찮아?

045

Would[Do] you mind if I smoke here?

여기서 담배펴도 돼요?

Would[Do] you mind ~ing[if]~? …해 줄래요?, …해도 돼요?

046

Would[Do] you mind if I go now?

지금 가도 될까요?

047

I was wondering if I could get a ride home with you

집까지 같이 타고 가도 돼?

I was wondering if you[I] could ~? …할 수 있을지 모르겠네요?

048

I'm sorry to trouble you, but could I borrow a pen?

미안하지만, 펜 좀 빌려줄래요?

049

Let's leave now, if that's all right with you

네가 괜찮다면 지금 나가자

050

if you don't mind

네가 괜찮다면

051

if it's okay with you

당신이 좋다면, 괜찮다면

Chapter **14**

상황별 영어
대표문장

COMMON
SENTENCES
IN SITUATION
ENGLISH

03 제안

4 상대방에게 뭔가 갖다 줄지 의향을 물어보기

052
Can I get you something?

뭐 좀 사다줄까?, 뭐 좀 갖다줄까?

053
Can I get you anything?

내가 뭐 사다줄[갖다줄] 거라도 있어?

054
Can I get you some coffee?

커피 좀 갖다줄까?

055
Can I get you another glass of wine?

와인 한 잔 더 갖다드릴까요?

056
What can I get for you?

뭘 갖다 줄까?

057
I('ve) got something for you

네게 줄 게 있어

058
I got this for you

이거 너 줄거야

059
Here's something for you
이거 너 줄려고

060
This is for you
널 위해 준비했어, 이건 네 거야

5 상대방에게 뭔가 하자고 제안하거나 권유하기

061
Why don't you ask for her number?
전화번호를 물어봐

Why don't you + 동사? …해라

062
Why don't we head over to the mall and do some shopping?
쇼핑센터가서 쇼핑하자

Why don't we +동사? …을 하자

063
You should get her a present
걔한테 선물해줘라

ou should + 동사 …해라

064
Let's go to the coffee shop around the corner
모퉁이 커피숍으로 갑시다

Let's + 동사 …하자

065

How about we have one more beer?

맥주 한 잔 더 하는 게 어때?

How about + ~ing[명사; 주어+동사]? …하는 게 어때? How about 다음에는 동사의 ~ing 형이나 명사만 오는 것이 아니라 '주어+동사'의 절의 형태로도 많이 쓰인다.

066

Shall we say around seven?

7시로 할까요?

Shall we ~? …할까요?

067

Would you like to begin after a short break?

잠시 쉬었다가 시작할래?

Would you like[care] to + 동사 ? …할래?

068

Would you like me to read them to everyone?

사람들에게 읽어줄까요?

Would you like me to + 동사 ~? 내가 …해줄까?

069

Do you want to come over to my place tonight?

오늘 밤 우리 집에 올래?

Do you want to + 동사~? …할래

070

Do you want me to give you a ride to the airport?

내가 공항까지 태워다 줄까?

Do you want me to + 동사~ ? 내가 …할까?

071
How would you like to get together? Say next Monday?

만나는 게 어때? 담주 월요일로?

How would you like to + 동사~? …하는 게 어때?

072
I wouldn't surf the Internet during business hours if I were you

나라면 근무시간 중에는 인터넷을 하지 않겠어

If I were in your situation[shoes], I would + 동사~ 너의 입장이라면 …할텐데. If I were you, I would+동사 '내가 너라면 난 …할텐데.' If it were me, I would+동사 '나라면 난 …할 텐데'도 많이 쓰이는 형태.

073
It'd be smart to work hard to get promoted

승진하려면 열심히 일하는 게 현명해

It would be smart to + 동사 …하는 게 좋을 걸

074
I have an idea

내게 생각이 있어

075
I have come up with an idea

좋은 생각이 하나 떠올랐어

076
I have a good idea

내게 좋은 생각이 있어

077 I suggest that you present a speech at the next conference

다음 회의에서 네가 발표해라

I suggest 주어+동사 …을 해봐, …을 제안할게

078 I want to make a suggestion

제안 하나 할게

079 Won't you join us?

우리랑 함께 할래?

080 We might as well go home now

지금 집에 가는게 나아

We might as well + 동사 …하는 게 나아

Chapter

15

의사소통

1 상대방과 잠시 얘기 좀 하자고 할 때

001 # Can I talk to you for a second?

잠깐 얘기 좀 할까?

002 # Can I talk to you for a minute?

잠깐 얘기 좀 할까?

003 # Can I tell you something?

말씀 좀 드려도 될까요?

004 # Can we talk?

얘기 좀 할까?

005 # Can we have a talk?

얘기 좀 할까?

006 # Can[May] I have a word (with you)?

잠깐 얘기 좀 할까?

007 # I want to talk to you (about that)

얘기 좀 하자고

008 # I gotta talk to you

할 얘기가 있어

009 # We need to talk (about that)

우리 얘기 좀 하자

010 # We have to talk

얘기 좀 하자

011 # Let's talk

같이 이야기해보자

Chapter **15**

012 # We'll talk later

나중에 이야기 하죠

013 # Let's talk about it[you]

그 문제[너]에 대해 얘기해보자

014 # Can I (just) ask you a question?

질문 하나 해도 될까?

015 # Let me ask you a question

뭐 하나 물어보자

016 # I have a question for you

질문 있는데요

017 # Let me ask you something

뭐 좀 물어볼게, 뭐 좀 부탁할게

018 # Let me ask you one thing

뭐 하나 물어보자

019 # Let me get back to you (on that)

나중에 이야기합시다, 생각해보고 다시 말해줄게

020 # I'll get back to you (on that)

나중에 이야기하자고

2 말 꺼내기에 앞서 가볍게 던지는 말들

021 # Look at this

이것 좀 봐

022 # Look here

이것 봐

023 Well
어, 저기

024 So
그래서

025 Look
저기

026 Anyway
어쨌든, 좌우간

027 By the way
참, 그런데, 참고로, 덧붙여서

028 You know
저 말야

029 As you know
너도 알다시피

030 Let me (just) say
말하자면, 글쎄

031

Let me see

그러니까 (내 생각엔), 저기

뒤에 명사나 절이 나오면 「…보자」, 「생각해보자」라는 의미가 된다.

032

As I mentioned before

내가 전에 말했듯이

033

As I said before

전에 말했다시피

034

How should I put it?

뭐랄까?

035

Put it another way

달리 표현하자면

036

How can I say this?

글쎄, 이걸 어떻게 말하죠?

3 말하려는 내용을 강조하려고 먼저 꺼내는 말

037

You know what?

그거 알아?, 근데 말야?

038 Guess what?

저기 말야?, 그거 알아?

039 I'll tell you what

이럼 어때, 이러면 어떨까, 있잖아

040 Tell you what

있지

041 Let me tell you something

내 생각은 말야, 내 말해두는데

042 I have to tell you (something)

말할게 있는데, (솔직히) 할 말이 있어

043 I have to[gotta] tell you this

이 말은 해야겠는데요

044 (Do) You know something?

그거 알아?

045 (Do you) (want to) Know something?

궁금하지 않아?

Chapter 15

046 I'm telling you

정말이야, 잘 들어

047 I'm telling you that you'll regret it

정말이지 너 후회하게 될거야.

I'm telling you 주어+동사   정말이지…

048 You won't believe this

이거 믿지 못할 걸

049 You're not gonna believe this

넌 못 믿을 걸, 믿기지 않을거야

050 You'll never guess what I heard

내가 들은 얘기는 넌 짐작도 못할거야

051 Do you know about this?

이거 아니?

052 Have you heard?

얘기 들었어?

053 Did you hear?

너 얘기 들었니?

054

Last but not least,

끝으로 중요한 말씀을 더 드리자면,

---

4 **꺼내기 어려운 이야기를 할 때**

055

Sorry I didn't tell you this before but I'm no longer at my job

미리 말 안해 미안하지만, 난 실직했어

I'm sorry I didn't tell you this before, but~ 전에 말하지 않아 미안하지만…

056

I don't know how to tell you this, but I think your wife's cheating on you

뭐라 얘기해야 할지 모르겠지만 네 아내 바람피고 있어.

I don't know how to tell you this, but~ 어떻게 이걸 말해야 할지 모르겠지만…

057

I'm afraid to say this, but you're not going to get a raise

말하기 좀 그렇지만 너 임금동결야

I'm afraid to say this, but~ 이런 말 하기 좀 미안하지만…

058

I've never told you this, but I'm not good at numbers

전에 말한 적 없지만 숫자에 약해

I've never told you this, but~ 전에 말한 적이 없지만…

059 I don't know if I've told you this, but I'm rich

이걸 말했는지 모르겠지만, 나 부자야

I don't know if I've told you this, but~ 내가 이걸 말했는지 모르겠지만…

060 If (my) memory serves me correctly[right]

내 기억이 맞다면

061 That reminds me

그러고 보니 생각나네

062 That rings a bell

얼핏 기억이 나네요

063 Rumor has it that you'll be transferred to New York

소문듣자니 뉴욕으로 전근간다며

Rumor has it (that) 주어+동사 …라는 소문을 들었어

064 A little bird told me

소문으로 들었어

065 I heard through the grapevine that you're going to get married

네가 결혼할거라는 소문을 들었어

I heard through the grapevine that~ …라는 것을 풍문으로 들었다

066
I got wind of it
그 얘기를 들었어, 그런 얘기가 있더라

067
I'm probably out of line here
이렇게 말해도 좋을지 모르겠지만

068
I have a confession to make
고백할 게 하나 있어

5 상대방이 말을 하도록 유도하는 표현들

069
Tell me something
말 좀 해봐

070
Tell me what you're thinking
네 생각이 뭔지 말해봐

071
So, tell me
자, 말해봐

072
Let's have it
어서 말해봐, 내게 줘

073 Just try me

나한테 한번 (얘기)해봐, 기회를 한번 줘봐

074 Like what?

예를 들면?

075 Such as?

예를 들면?

076 What else is new?

뭐 더 새로운 소식은 없어?

077 Anything else?

다른 건 없니?

078 You were saying?

당신 말은?, 그래서?

079 Please go on

계속해봐

6 하려는 말이 기억이 나지 않을 때

080
It completely slipped my mind
깜박 잊었어

081
It's on the tip of my tongue
혀 끝에서 뱅뱅 도는데

082
I was somewhere else
잠시 딴 생각했어요

083
I totally forgot
까맣게 잊어버렸어

084
I just forgot
그냥 잊었어

085
Where was I?
내가 무슨 얘길 했더라?, 내가 어디까지 이야기했더라?

086
Where were we?
우리 어디까지 얘기했지?

087 What was I saying?

내가 무슨 말하고 있었지?

088 The cat got your tongue?

왜 말이 없어?

이해

7 상대방 말을 잘 듣지 못해 다시 말해달라고 할 때

089

Excuse me?

뭐라고?

090

Excuse me, I didn't hear

미안하지만 잘 못들어서

091

I can't hear you (well)

(잘) 못들었어

092

I'm sorry?

예?, 뭐라고?

093

Come again?

뭐라구요?

094

Say it again?

뭐라구요?, 다시 한번 말해줄래요?

095

Say it once more, please

한 번 더 말해주세요

096 Pardon me?

죄송하지만 뭐라고 하셨어요?

097 Pardon?

뭐라고요?

098 I beg your pardon?

뭐라고 하셨죠?

099 What was that again?

뭐라고 했어요?

100 What did you say?

뭐라고 했는데?, 뭐라고?

101 Say what?

뭐라고? 다시 말해줄래?

102 Says who?

누가 그래?, 누가 어쨌다구?

103 Would you speak slower, please?

조금 천천히 말씀해줄래요?

104 Could[Would] you please repeat that?

다시 한번 말해줄래요?

105 Tell her what?

그녀에게 뭐라고 하라고?

106 You're what?

뭐하고 있다고?, 뭐라고?

107 You did what?

네가 뭐 어쨌다구?

108 You did it when?

언제 그랬다구?

109 Who did what?

누가 무엇을 했다고?

110 You did?

그랬어?

111 You do?

아 그래?

112 You are?

그래?

113 You were?

그랬어?

114 You have?

그래?

8 상대방 말을 이해못해 다시 말해달라고 할 때

115 What do you mean?

그게 무슨 말이야?

116 What does it mean?

그게 무슨 뜻이야?

117 I'm not sure what you mean

무슨 말인지 모르겠어

118 What do you mean by that?

그게 무슨 말이야?

119
What do you mean you quit? You can't quit!

그만둔다는 게 무슨 말야? 안돼!

What do you mean 주어+ 동사? …라는 게 무슨 의미죠?

120
What's your[the] point?

요점이 뭔가?, 하고 싶은 말이 뭔가?

121
What are you driving at?

말하려는게 뭐야?

122
What are you getting at?

뭘 말하려는거야?

123
I don't know what you're getting at

무슨 말 하려는건지 모르겠어

124
What are you talking about?

무슨 소리야?

125
I'm not sure what you're talking about

네가 무슨 얘기를 하는지 잘 모르겠어

126
What's the bottom line?

요점이 뭐야?

127 What's the catch?

속셈이 뭐야?, 무슨 꿍꿍이야?

128 What are you trying to say?

무슨 말을 하려는거야?

129 I don't get it[that]

모르겠어, 이해가 안돼

130 I didn't quite get that

잘 이해가 안돼

131 I can't get it right

제대로 이해 못하겠어

132 I didn't catch that

그 말을 못 알아들었어요

133 I didn't catch what you just said

네 말이 무슨 뜻인지 모르겠어

134 You lost me

못 알아듣겠는데

You lost me (back) at ~ …부터는 무슨 얘긴지 모르겠어

135 I can't follow you

무슨 말인지 모르겠어

136 I can't see your point

무슨 말하는지 모르겠어

137 That's not clear

분명하지가 않아

9 상대방의 말을 이해했다고 말할 때

138 I know what you mean

무슨 의미인지 알아

139 I know what you're saying

무슨 말인지 알아

140 That's what I'm saying

내 말이 그 말이야

141 I got it

알았어

142 I get the idea

알겠어

143 I get the picture

알겠어

144 You got it

맞아, 바로 그거야, 알았어

145 I get your point

무슨 말인지 알아들었어, 알겠어요

146 I (can) see your point

네 말을 알겠어

147 I can see that

알겠어, 알고 있어요

148 So I figured it out

그래서 (연유를) 알게 되었지

149 Say no more

더 말 안해도 돼, 알았어 무슨 말인지

150 **We're talking the same language**

이제 얘기가 된다

151 **You're speaking my language**

이제 얘기가 되는 구만

152 **We're not speaking the same language**

말이 안 통하는군

153 **Now you're talking**

그래 바로 그거야!, 그렇지!

154 **Bingo**

바로 그거야

155 **You took the words right out of my mouth**

내가 하고 싶은 말이야

156 **You're getting it!**

이제 알아듣는 구만!

157 **Am I getting warm?**

(정답 등에) 가까워지고 있는 거야?

158 Not even close

어림도 없어

159 You came close!

(퀴즈 등) 거의 다 맞췄어!

10 상대방의 말이 이치에 맞거나 납득이 가는 경우에

160 That makes sense

일리가 있어

161 That does make sense

그건 정말 일리가 있는 말이야

162 That figures

그럴 줄 알았어, 그럼 그렇지

163 That explains it

그럼 설명이 되네, 아 그래서 이런 거구나

164 No wonder

당연하지

¹⁶⁵ **It all adds up**

앞뒤가 들어 맞아

¹⁶⁶ **I knew it**

그럴 줄 알았어

¹⁶⁷ **It is just as I imagined**

내 생각했던 대로야

¹⁶⁸ **It's just like I dreamed**

내가 생각했던 거와 똑같아

Chapter 15

¹⁶⁹ **See? I told you**

거봐? 내가 뭐랬어

¹⁷⁰ **See? I told you so**

거봐? 내가 그랬잖아

¹⁷¹ **See? I'm right**

거봐? 내가 맞잖아

¹⁷² **See? Didn't I tell you so?**

거봐? 내가 그러지 않았어?

COMMON
SENTENCES
IN SITUATION
ENGLISH

173 I said that, didn't I?

내가 그랬지, 안그래?

174 You see that?

봤지?, 내 말이 맞지?

175 That's why I decided to quit

그래서 내가 그만 두려고 하는 거야

That's why 주어+동사 그래서 …하는 거야

176 That's because I didn't want you to come!

네가 오길 원치 않으니까!

That's because 주어+동사 그건 …때문이야

11 상대방이 이해를 제대로 했는지 물어보기

177 You got it?

알았어?

178 You got that?

알아 들었어?

179 You got that, right?

제대로 알아 들었어?

(Do) You know what I mean?

무슨 말인지 알겠어?

(Do) You know what I'm saying?

무슨 얘기인지 알겠어?

(Do) You understand what I'm saying?

내 말 이해돼요?

See what I'm saying?

무슨 말인지 알지?

You know what I'm talking about?

내 말이 무슨 말인지 알아?

Are you with me?

내 말 이해 돼?, 내 편이 돼줄테야?

Are you following me?

알아듣고 있지?

Do you follow me?

내 말 아시겠죠?

188 Do I make myself clear?

내 말이 무슨 말인지 알겠어?

189 Am I making myself understood?

제 말이 잘 전달되었는지 모르겠어요

190 I didn't make myself clear

제 말 뜻을 이해하지 못하셨군요

191 Am I getting through on this?

이 문제에 관해서는 내 말을 잘 알겠지?

192 (Do) You get the picture?

너 이해했어?

193 Get the message?

알아들었어?

194 Understood?

알았어?

195 Do you understand?

이해했어?

196 Is that clear?

분명히 알겠어?

197 Do you read me?

내 말 들려?, 무슨 말인지 알겠어?

198 (Do you) See?

알겠어?

12 상대방을 이해시키기 위해 들어보라고 말할 때

199 (You) Listen to me!

내 말 좀 들어봐!

200 Are you listening to me?

듣고 있어?

201 You don't seem to be listening

안 듣는 것 같은데

202 You're just not listening

딴 짓하고 있네

203

Hear me out

내 말 끝까지 들어봐

204

I'm talking to you!

내가 하는 말 좀 잘 들어봐!

205

Stay with me

끝까지 들어봐

206

That's not the end of the story

얘기가 끝난 게 아냐

207

How many times do I have to tell you?

도대체 몇번을 말해야 알겠어?

208

If I've told you once, I've told you a thousand times

한 번만 더 얘기하면 천번 째다

209

I'm listening

듣고 있어, 어서 말해

210

I'm not listening to you

난 네 말 안 듣는다고

211 They're not listening to me

걔네들이 내 말 들으려고 하지도 않아

212 I am all ears

귀 쫑긋 세우고 들을게

213 She was all ears

그 여자는 열심히 경청했다

13 비밀을 이야기 할 때

214 This is just between you and me

이건 우리끼리 이야기야

215 It's a secret

비밀야

216 This is for your eyes only

이건 너만 알고 있어야 돼

217 Keep your mouth shut(~)

(…에 대해) 누구한테도 말하면 안돼

COMMON
SENTENCES
IN SITUATION
ENGLISH

218 Mum's the word

입 꼭 다물고 있어

219 Don't tell anyone my secret!

아무한테도 말하지마!

220 Could you keep a secret?

비밀로 해주실래요?

221 Your secret's safe with me

비밀 지켜드릴게요

222 My lips are sealed

입다물고 있을게요

223 I won't say a word

한 마디도 안 할게

224 I'll take it to my grave

그 얘기 무덤까지 가지고 가마

225 I won't breathe a word (of it)

입도 뻥긋 안 할게

226 It was a slip of the tongue

내가 실언했네

227 I spoke out of turn

말이 잘못 나왔어, 내가 잘못 말했어

228 I let the cat out of the bag

비밀이 들통났어

229 I didn't say anything

난 아무 말도 안했어

230 That's an open secret now

지금은 다 공공연한 비밀인데

14 상대방과 오해를 풀거나 오해를 방지하고플 때

231
I didn't mean it
고의로 그런 건 아냐

232
I didn't mean any harm
마음 상하게 할 생각은 없었어

233
I really didn't mean any offense
기분상하게 할려는 건 아니었는데

234
I didn't mean to offend you
기분 상하게 할 의도는 아니었어

235
That's not what I mean
실은 그런 뜻이 아냐

236
That's not what I said
내 말은 그런 게 아냐

237
I'm sorry, I meant to say thank you
미안하지만 네게 고맙다고 말할 생각이었어

I'm sorry, I meant to + 동사～ 미안하지만 …할 생각이었어

238 Don't get me wrong

오해하지마

239 You've got it all wrong

잘못 알고 있는거야

240 There're no hard[ill] feelings (on my part)

악의는 아냐, 기분 나쁘게 생각하지마

241 No offense

악의는 없었어, 기분 나빠하지마

242 Don't take it personally

기분 나쁘게 받아들이지마

243 Don't take this wrong

잘못 받아들이지마

15 오해를 막기 위해 서로의 의도를 정확히 할 때

244 Do you mean you won't be coming over for dinner?

저녁 먹으러 못 온다고?

Do you mean~? …란 말야?

 Chapter 15

245

You mean you're not going to come over?

못 온다는 말이지?

You mean,~ 네 말은…

246

Let me make sure I understand. You don't love her?

제대로 알아들었는지 확인해볼게. 아내를 사랑하지 않는다고?

Let me make sure~ 확실히 하자면 …란 말이지

247

Let me get this straight

이건 분명히 해두자, 얘기를 정리해보자고

248

We need to get this straight

이건 분명히 해둬야 돼

249

Let's just get one thing straight

이거 하나는 분명히 해두죠

250

That isn't the way I heard it

내가 들은 이야기랑 다르네

251

You're just saying that

그냥 해보는 소리지, 괜한 소리지

252
You're just saying that because you're my biggest fan

나의 열렬한 팬이니까 그러는거지

You're just saying 주어+동사 그냥 …라고 하는 거지

253
Would you please be more specific?

좀 더 구체적으로 말씀해줄래요?

254
Are you saying that it's a bad idea?

그게 나쁜 생각이라고 하는거지?

Are you saying that~? …라는 거지?

255
Are you trying to say that this book is wrong?

이 책은 안좋다고 말하려는거야?

Are you trying to say that~? …라고 말하려는거야?

16 내가 말하는 내용을 다시 한번 분명히 말할 때

256
That's my point

내 말이 그거야

257
That's not the point

핵심은 그게 아니라고

258
What I'm trying to say is we're short-handed

내 말은 일손이 부족하다는거야

What I'm trying to say 주어+동사 내가 말하고자 하는 건…

259
What I'd like to say is that you're not qualified for this job

내가 말하고 싶은 건 당신은 이 일에 자격이 안 된다는 겁니다

What I'd like to say is that 주어+동사 내가 말하고 싶은 건…

260
What I'm saying is we have to work overtime this week

내 말은 이번 주 야근해야 된다는거야

What I'm saying is 주어+동사 내가 말하는 건…

261
What I said was we have to work overtime this week

내 말은 이번 주 야근해야 된다는거야

What I said was 주어+동사 내가 말한 건…

262
I mean, I don't like to be with you

내 말은, 너하고 함께 하고 싶지 않아

I mean,~ 내 말은…

263
I'm just saying that we should get together more often

그냥 우리가 자주 만나야 된다는거야

I'm just saying (that) 주어+동사 내 말은 단지 …라는거야

17 상대방에게 숨기지 말고 솔직히 말하자고 할 때

264

Be honest

솔직히 털어놔

265

You have to be honest with me

너 나한테 솔직히 말해

266

I'll be honest with you

네게 솔직히 털어놓을게

267

Level with me

솔직히 말해봐

268

I'll level with you

솔직히 말할게

269

Tell me the truth

사실대로 말해

270

You've got to come clean with me!

나한테 실토해!

271 Give it to me straight

솔직히 말해봐

272 Don't beat around the bush

말 돌리지 마, 핵심을 말해

273 Let's cut to the chase

단도직입적으로 물어볼게

叫 확인

18 상대방의 말이 놀랍거나 혹은 못 믿겠을 때

274 Are you serious?
정말이야?, 농담 아냐?

275 Are you for real?
정말이야?

276 Are you sure (about that)?
정말이야?

277 Is that true[right]?
정말이야?

278 Is that so?
확실해?, 정말 그럴까?

279 You mean it?
정말야?

280 Do you mean that?
정말야?

COMMON
SENTENCES
IN SITUATION
ENGLISH

281 # You're kidding!
농담하지마!, 장난하는거지!

282 # Are you kidding?
농담하는 거야?, 무슨 소리야?

283 # No kidding!
설마!, 너 농담하냐!, 진심야!

284 # You're not kidding
정말 그렇네

285 # Is this some kind of joke?
장난하는거지?

286 # You must be joking
농담하는거지

287 # Did I hear you right?
정말이니?, 내가 제대로 들은 거야?

288 # Get out of here!
농담하지마!

289 ## Really?

정말?

290 ## Oh yeah?

어, 그래?

291 ## You bet!

정말!

19 ### 내가 말하는 내용이 진심임을 확인해 줄 때

292 ## I mean it

진심이야

293 ## I mean business

진심이야

294 ## I don't mean maybe!

장난 아냐!

295 ## I'm not kidding

정말이야, 장난 아냐

296 I kid you not

장난삼아 하는 말 아냐

297 I'm telling the truth

진짜야

298 I'm not lying

정말이라니까

299 I am (dead) serious

(정말) 진심이야

300 I'll bet

틀림없어, 정말이야, 확실해, 그러겠지

기본적으로 I'll bet은 상대방의 말에 수긍하는 표현이지만 "그러겠지," "어련하시겠어"라는 빈정대는 뜻으로도 쓰인다.

301 I bet (you)

맹세해

302 I'll bet you

내 너한테 맹세하마

303 I'd bet my life on it

그건 내가 맹세해

304 I'll say

정말이야

305 You can bet on it

그럼, 물론이지

306 You can bet she wants to go

걔가 가고 싶어하는게 틀림없어

You can bet 주어+동사 …인 게 틀림없어

307 Believe me

정말이야

308 Believe you me

정말 진심이야

309 How true

정말 그렇다니까

20 내 말이 진심이니 믿어달라고 하소연하기

310 Take my word for it

진짜야, 믿어줘

311 You have my word

내 약속하지

312 I give you my word

약속할게

313 Mark my words!

내 말 잘 들어!

314 (You can) Trust me

믿어봐

315 You'd better believe it

맞아, 정말야

316 I promise (you)!

정말이야

I promise와 I promise you는 같은 의미이지만 I promise you의 의미가 다소 강함.

317 Promise?

약속하는 거지?

318 I swear

맹세해

319 I swear to God[you]

하나님께[네게] 맹세코

320 I swear I told you all about it

맹세코 다 얘기한 거라니까

321 Believe what I say

내 말 믿어줘

322 You can take it from me

그 점은 내 말을 믿어도 돼

323 Have faith in me

날 믿어줘

324 It may sound strange, but it's true

이상하게 들리겠지만 진짜야

21 상대방에게 이유를 물어볼 때

325 How come?

어째서?, 왜?

326 How come you're late?

어쩌다 이렇게 늦은거야?

How come 주어+동사? 왜 …하는 거야?

327 What makes you think so?

왜 그렇게 생각하니?, 꼭 그런건 아니잖아?

328 What makes you so mad?

뭐 때문에 그렇게 화난거야?

329 How did it happen?

이게 어떻게 된 거야?

330 What brings you here?

무슨 일로 왔어?

331 What for?

왜요?, 뭣 때문에?

332 For what?

왜?, 뭣 때문에?

333 What're you doing this for?

왜 그러는 거야?

What ~ for? 어째서…?, 무엇 때문에…?

334 Why do you think that?

왜 그렇게 생각하는거야?

335 Why do you say that?

왜 그렇게 말하는거야?

336 Why did you do that?

왜 그랬어?

337 Why would you say that?

왜 그런 말을 하는거야?

338 What's the reason?

이유가 뭔대?

339 Tell me why

이유를 말해봐

340 I was just wondering

그냥 물어봤어

Common Sentences
in Situation English

Chapter

16

생각 · 의견

01 생각
02 기호
03 관심

 **01** 생각

① 내 생각 꺼낼 때 하는 말들

001

The way I see it

내가 보기엔

002

As far as I can see

내가 보기엔

003

As I see it, we need to save more money

내가 보기로는 좀 더 저축해야 돼

As I see it 내가 보기로는

004

The way I look at it is that we have to wait until he's back

걔가 돌아올 때까지 기다려야 할 것 같아

The way I look at it is~ 내가 보기엔 …이야

005

The thing is I need to find a date

중요한 건 데이트 상대를 찾아야 된다는거야

The thing is (that) 주어+동사 중요한 건 …라는 거야

006

The point is that we are bankrupt

요점은 우리가 파산했다는 겁니다

The point is that 주어+동사 요점은 …라는 것이야

007
My opinion in a nutshell is that he will win the race

내 의견은 한마디로 경주에서 걔가 이길거라는 거야

My opinion in a nutshell is that 주어+동사 내 의견은 한마디로 …이야

008
I (will) tell you what I think

내 생각을 말하면 이래

009
This is what we'll do

우리 이렇게 하자

010
Here's my plan

내 생각은 이래

011
Here's my idea

내 생각 들어봐

012
Here's the deal

이렇게 하자, 이런 거야

013
Here's the thing

내 말인 즉은, 그게 말야, 문제가 되는 건

014 **If you ask me**

내 생각은, 내 생각을 말한다면

2 내 생각을 말하기

015 **I think it would be better if you went to bed**

잠자러 가는 게 좋을 것 같은데

I think~ …것 같아

016 **I guess he got the contract**

내 생각에는 걔가 계약을 따낸 것 같아

I guess~ …인 것 같아

017 **It seems like that I have lost my wallet**

지갑을 잃어버린 듯해요

It seems (like) that~ …인 것 같은데

018 **I feel like my head is going to explode!**

머리가 폭발할 것 같아!

I feel like 주어+동사 …할 것 같아

019 **It looks like you don't like your meal at all**

밥이 네 입맛에 전혀 맞지 않나 보구나

It looks like[as if]~ …처럼 보여

020
It sounds like you need a new mouse

새 마우스가 필요할 것 같은데

It sounds like~ …한 것 같아

021
I'm afraid I don't know what to say

뭐라고 해야 할지 모르겠어

022
I doubt that they'll know what to do

걔들이 뭘 해야 하는 지 모를걸

023
I doubt you'll be able to get soccer tickets

네가 표를 못 구할 것 같아

I doubt~ 과연 …일까 의심스러워

024
I suspect that my son has been smoking

웬지 우리 아들이 담배피우는 것 같아

I suspect~ 아무래도 …인 것 같아

025
I have a feeling that they are not going to show up

걔들이 안 올 것 같아

I have a feeling ~ …인 것 같아

026
I have a hunch that he's lying

걔가 거짓말하는 것 같아

I have a hunch that~ …라는 느낌이 들어

027 # I bet you will find a new boyfriend soon

곧 틀림없이 새로운 남친을 만나게 될거야

I bet 주어+동사 난 틀림없이 …라고 생각해

028 # Fine, then let's just say she's not my type

좋아, 그럼 걘 내 타입이 아닌 것 같아

Let's just say 주어+동사 …라고 생각해

3 상대방의 생각이나 의견을 물어보기(1)

029 # How[What] about you?

네 생각은 어때?

030 # How about it?

그거 어때?

031 # What do you think?

네 생각은 어때?, 무슨 말이야? / 그걸 말이라고 해?

032 # What do you think of[about] that?

넌 그걸 어떻게 생각해?

033 # What do you think will happen?

어떻게 될 것 같아?

What do you think~? 어떻게 …를 생각해?

034
What is your opinion?

네 의견은 어때?

035
What is your feeling about this?

여기에 대해 네 생각은 어때?

036
What do you think is the best?

뭐가 최선인 것 같아?

037
Which is better, getting married or being single?

결혼과 싱글 중 어떤 게 좋아?

Which is better, A or B? A와 B중에서 어떤 게 좋아?

038
Is it 'yes' or 'no?'

그렇다는거야 안 그렇다는거야?

039
Yes or no?

찬성야 반대야?

040
Does it work for you?

네 생각은 어때?, 너도 좋아?

041 **Do you like it?**
좋았어?

042 **Did you have fun?**
재밌었어?

043 **Don't you think so?**
그렇게 생각되지 않아?

044 **Like this?**
이렇게 하면 돼?

4 상대방의 생각이나 의견을 물어보기(2)

045 **How was it?**
어땠어?

046 **How did you like it?**
어땠어?

047 **How'd it go?**
어떻게 됐어?, 어땠어?

048 How did it go at the doctor's?

병원에 간 일은 어땠어?

049 How do you like this suit?

이 옷 어때?

How would you like + 명사~? ···는 어때요?, 어떻게 (준비) 해드릴까요?
How would you like 다음에 'to+동사'가 오면 권유의 문장으로 「···하는 게 어때?」라는 의미이다.

050 How would you like it if we switched offices?

사무실을 바꾸면 어떻겠어?

How would you like it if 주어+동사~? ···한다면 어떻겠어?

051 What do you say?

어때?

052 What do you say to going for a drink tonight?

오늘 밤 한잔 하러 가는 거 어때요?

What do you say to + 명사[동사~ing]? ···하는 게 어때?

053 What do you say that we eat some lunch?

점심 좀 먹는 게 어때?

What do you say (that) 주어+동사? ···어때요?

054 What would you say?

어떻게 할거야?, 넌 뭐라고 할래?

055

What would you say if I wanted to stay home?

내가 집에 더 있는 건 어떨까?

What would you say if 주어+동사~? …한다면 어떨까?

02 기호

5 내가 좋아한다고 말할 때

056 I like that

그거 좋은데, 맘에 들어

would를 삽입해서 I'd like that하면 "그러면 좋겠다." "그렇게 한다면 난 좋다"라는 표현으로 상대방의 제안이나 권유에 찬성을 뜻하는 표현이 된다.

057 I love it!

정말 좋다, 내 맘에 꼭들어!

058 I began to like Bulgogi

불고기를 좋아하게 됐어

059 I've started to like Pasta

파스타를 좋아하기 시작했어

060 I like tea better than coffee

차보다는 커피가 좋아

I like A better than B 난 B보다 A가 좋아

061 I think I prefer Suwon to other cities in Korea

한국에서 수원이 타도시보다 더 좋아

I prefer A to B 난 B보다 A가 좋아

062 I'm fond of reading novels

소설 읽는 걸 좋아해

063 I want a straight answer

분명한 답을 듣고 싶어

I want + 명사 …를 원해, 필요해

064 I want to get her number

전화번호를 알아내고 싶은 걸

I want to + 동사 …하기를 원해, …해야 해

065 I'd like a round-trip ticket to New York

뉴욕행 왕복항공권을 주세요

I'd like + 명사 …를 원해

066 I'd like to go out for lunch on Friday

금요일에 같이 점심 먹으러 갔으면 하는데

I'd like to + 동사 …했으면 해

067 I'd love to go, but I've got too much work to do

가고 싶지만, 할 일이 많아

I'd love to + 동사 …하고 싶어

068 I'd love it if you would do it

네가 그걸 한다면 좋지

I'd love it if~ …하면 좋을텐데

069 I need the money

돈이 필요해

I need + 명사 …가 필요해

070 I need to take the rest of the day off

오늘은 그만 쉬어야겠어요

I need to + 동사 …해야 해

071 I feel like having a nice cold beer right now

지금 시원한 맥주가 당기는데

I feel like ~ing …가 하고 싶어

072 I can't wait to see the results of the test

시험 성적을 알고 싶어 죽겠어

I can't wait (to+동사) 지금 당장이라고 하고 싶어

Chapter 16

073 I'm willing to pay as much as 2,000 dollars for it

2천달러 정도 낼 의향이 있어

I'm willing to + 동사 기꺼이 …하고 싶어

074 I'm looking forward to doing it

무척 기다려져

075 You up for it?

하고 싶어?

076 I'm just not up for it tonight

오늘 밤에는 생각없어

077 I'm eager to start my vacation

어서 휴가를 갔으면 해

I'm eager to + 동사 …를 무지 하고 싶어

078 I'm dying to meet her

걔를 만나고 싶어 죽겠어

I'm dying to + 동사 …하고 싶어 죽겠어

079 I'm itching to go travelling again

다시 여행 가고 싶어서 견딜 수가 없어

I'm itching to + 동사 몹시 …하고 싶어

080 Hopefully!

바라건대, 그랬음 좋겠다!

081 Good enough!

딱 좋아!

082 Well, I'm a real fan of Manchester United

음, 난 맨유가 정말 좋아

I'm a real fan of~ 난 …를 정말 좋아해

6 내가 싫어한다고 말하기

083
I don't like it
싫어해

084
I hate it
싫어해

085
I'm not into it
그런 건 안해요

086
I don't want to get involved
끼어들고 싶지 않아

087
I'm not going to be part of it
난 끼고 싶지 않아

088
That's not for me
내 것이 아닌데, 그런 건 나한테는 안 어울려

089
I don't care for it
난 싫어

090

That's not my cup of tea

내 취향이 아냐

091

That's not my thing

난 그런 건 질색이야

092

The last thing I want to do is lay anyone off

누굴 해고한다는 게 가장 싫은 일야

The last thing I want to do is 주어+동사 가장 하고 싶지 않은 건 …이다

7 내가 바라거나 희망하는 내용을 말할 때

093

I hope you like it

네 맘에 들었으면 좋겠어

I hope 주어+동사~ …면 좋겠어

094

I hope to enroll in a course this summer

올 여름에 한 과목 등록하고 싶어

I hope to + 동사 …하기를 바래. I wish to 또한 「…하기를 바란다」이지만 I hope to에 비해 다분히 공식적인 경우에 쓰인다.

095

I hope so

그랬으면 좋겠어

096

I hope not

그러지 말았으면 좋겠다. 아니라면 좋을텐데

097

It would be nice if we could take a vacation

우리가 휴가를 얻는다면 좋을텐데

It would be nice if 주어+동사 …한다면 좋을 텐데

098

It'll be good to see my family again

가족을 다시 보는 건 멋질거야

It'll be good[nice: wonderful] to + 동사 …하면 멋질 거야

099

I'd rather play computer games than study

공부를 하느니 컴퓨터 게임을 할거야

I'd rather A than B A하느니 차라리 B할 거야

100

If only I could remember her name

그 여자 이름을 기억하면 좋겠는데

If only I could~ …할 수 있다면 좋을 텐데

101

I wish I had a little time for fun

놀 시간이 좀 있으면 좋겠어

I wish 주어+동사 …였으면 좋겠어

102

I wish you would get out of my face!

네가 꺼져줬으면 좋겠어!

103

If I had his phone number, I would call him

걔 전화번호를 알면 전화할텐데

If I + 과거, I would + 동사 …이면 …할 텐데

104   If I had never met my wife, this would never have happened

와이프를 만나지 않았더라면 이런 일이 생기지 않았을텐데

If I had + pp, I would[could; might] have + pp …였다면 …했을텐데

03 관심

8 내가 관심이 있거나 없음을 말할 때

105 It matters to me

그건 내게 중요한 문제야

106 It doesn't matter to me

난 아무래도 상관없어요

107 It doesn't matter

상관없어

108 I'm interested in the new yoga class

새로 생긴 요가교실에 관심이 있어

I'm (not) interested in~ …에 관심이 있(없)어

109 I really don't want to get involved in it

정말이지 거기 끼고 싶지 않아

I'm involved in~ …을 하고 있어

110 Thanks! I'm really into health food now

고마워! 요즘 건강식에 관심많아

I'm into~ 난 …에 관심이 많아

Chapter 16

111 I know, but nothing appeals to me today

그래, 하지만 오늘은 딱 끌리는 게 없어

Something appeals to me ···가 끌리다

112 I don't care (about it)

(상대방의 부탁, 제안에 대해 승낙하며) 상관없어

113 I don't care what they say

걔들이 뭐래든 상관없어

I don't care if[what: how much]~ 난 (뭐라도, 얼마나 ~해도) 상관없어

114 I couldn't care less

알게 뭐람

115 It makes no difference to me

상관없어

116 It doesn't make any difference

상관없어

117 It's not going to make any difference

전혀 상관없어

118 It's gonna make a difference

차이가 있을 거야

119 What's the difference?
그게 무슨 상관이야?

120 What difference does it make?
그게 무슨 차이야?

121 It doesn't mean anything to me
난 상관없어

122 It's not my concern[business]
난 관심없어

123 It's not my problem
나하고 상관없어

124 I have nothing to do with this
난 아무 관련이 없어

125 It doesn't have anything to do with me
난 모르는 일이야

126 Who cares?
누가 신경이나 쓴대?

127 So what?

그래서 뭐가 어쨌다고?

128 So shoot me

그래서 어쨌다는 거야

129 Whatever!

뭐든지 간에!

130 The hell with that

알게 뭐람! 맘대로 해

131 To hell with tradition

전통따위 알게 뭐람

132 I don't give a shit[damn, fuck]

난 알 바아냐

Common Sentences
in Situation English

Chapter

17

동의 · 반대

상황별 영어
대표문장

COMMON
SENTENCES
IN SITUATION
ENGLISH

01 긍정

1 상대방의 말에 가볍게 긍정하기

001

I'm afraid so

(안타깝게도) 그런 것 같아

002

I guess so

아마 그럴 걸

003

I think so

그래요

004

I believe so

그럴 거라 생각해

005

I suppose (so)

그럴 걸

006

It might be true

사실일 수도 있어

007

It could be

그럴 수도 있어

008 It's possible

그럴 수 있어

009 Sort[Kind] of

어느 정도는, 다소

010 Yes and no

글쎄 어떨지

011 Maybe yes, maybe no

어느 쪽이라고 말해야 할지

2 상대방의 말에 강하게 긍정할 때

012 Absolutely!

물론이지!

반대로 Absolutely not!하면 「물론 아니지」란 의미가 되며 비슷한 표현으로는 Certainly!(확실해!) – Certainly not!(정말 아냐!) 그리고 Definitely!(틀림없어!)– Definitely not!(절대 아냐!)이 있다.

013 Of course

물론이지, 확실해

014 Sure

물론, 당연하지

015 Sure thing

물론이지, 그럼

016 It sure is

그렇고 말고, 맞고 말고

017 That's for sure

확실하지, 물론이지

018 (It's) For sure

물론이야

019 No doubt

분명해

020 There is no doubt about it!

틀림없어!

021 You bet

확실해, 물론이지

022 **All right**

알았어

023 **All right, already!**

좋아 알았다구!, 이제 그만해라!

024 **All right then**

좋아 그럼

025 **All right, I get it**

좋아 알겠어

026 **All right, I see**

좋아 알았어

027 **Okay**

좋아

Okay나 All right은 상대방의 말에 동의하는 표현이며, That's okay나 That's all right은 역시
상대방의 말에 동의하는 표현으로도 쓰이지만 상대방의 사과에 괜찮다는 「용서의 표현」으로도 쓰
인다. 이때는 No problem과 의미가 유사하다.

028 **Okey-dokey [Okie-dokie]**

좋아, 됐어

029 That's great

아주 좋아, 잘 됐어

030 That's nice

좋아, 잘했어

031 That's cool

좋아

032 That's terrific[wonderful]

끝내주네[훌륭해]

033 That's really something

거 굉장하네

034 I'd like that

그러면 좋겠다, 그렇게 한다면 난 좋다

035 That would be great[perfect]

그럼 좋겠어

036 (That) Sounds good (to me)

좋은데

037

Sounds great

아주 좋아

038

Sounds like a plan

좋은 생각이야

039

Sounds like fun

재밌을 것 같은데

040

Sounds interesting

재미있겠는데

041

Sounds like a good idea

좋은 생각 같은데

Chapter **17**

상황별 영어
대표문장

COMMON
SENTENCES
IN SITUATION
ENGLISH

02 동의

4 상대방의 말이 맞다고 맞장구 치기

042

That's right

맞아, 그래

043

You're right

네 말이 맞아

044

You're exactly right

정말 맞아

045

I think you're right (about that)

(그 점에 있어서) 네가 옳은 것 같아

046

You're right on the money

네 말이 맞아

047

That's a good point

좋은 지적이야, 맞는 말이야

048

You have a point there

네 말이 맞아

049 # You've got a point

맞는 말이다

050 # You got that right

네 말이 맞아

051 # That's correct

맞아

052 # You're correct

네가 맞아

053 # That's it

바로 그거야, 그게 다야, 그만두자

054 # That's it?

이걸로 끝이야?

055 # Tell me about it!

그 얘기 좀 해봐, 그게 맞아, 그렇고 말고!

056 # You're telling me!

누가 아니래!, 정말 그래!, 나도 알아!

057 Big time
그렇고 말고, 많이

058 In a word, yes
한마디로 말해서 그래

059 In a sense he's right
어떤 의미에서 걔 말이 맞아

5 상대방의 말에 동의하기

060 I agree
그래

061 I agree with you 100%
전적으로 동감이야

062 I couldn't agree with you more
정말 네 말이 맞아

063 I can't argue with that
두말하면 잔소리지, 물론이지

064
I can't disagree with you

네 말이 맞아

065
You can say that again

그렇고 말고, 당근이지

066
You could[might] say that

두말하면 잔소리지

067
You said it

네 말이 맞아

068
Well said

그 말 한번 잘했어, 맞는 말이야

Chapter 17

069
I'm with you

동감이야, 알았어

070
I'm with you there

나도 그 말에 공감해

071
I feel the same way

나도 그렇게 생각해

595

072 I'm like you

나도 너랑 같은 생각이야

073 We're on the same page

우린 같은 생각이야

074 I'm on your side

난 네 편이야

075 Same here

나도 그래

076 So am I

나도 그래

077 So do I

나도 그래

078 Go ahead

그렇게 해

079 Yes, please do

어, 그렇게 해

찬성

6 상대방의 말에 나도 그렇다라고 찬성하기

080
I'm for it
난 찬성이야

081
I'm for giving him another chance
걔에게 기회를 한 번 더 주는데 찬성야

082
I'm for the basic idea
기본적인 생각은 찬성야

083
I'm in favor of it
찬성이야

084
Let's do it
자 하자, 그러자

085
That's more like it
그게 더 낫겠어

086
I don't see why not
그래

087 **I'll drink to that!**

옳소!, 찬성이오!

088 **Why not?**

왜 안해?, 왜 안되는 거야?, 그러지 뭐

089 **A deal's a deal**

약속한 거야

090 **(It's a) Deal!**

그러기로 한 거야!, 내 약속하지!

091 **(It's a) Done deal**

그러기로 한 거야

092 **It's settled!**

그렇게 하자!

093 **I'm standing behind you**

내가 뒤에 있잖아

094 **I'll stand by you**

네 옆에 있어줄게

7 **가볍게 찬성하거나 허락하면서 상대방의 말을 받아주기**

095

That's all right

괜찮아, 됐어

고맙다는 혹은 미안하다는 말에 대한 답변으로 자주 쓰이는 표현

096

I'm all right with that

난 괜찮아

097

They seem all right with it

걔네들 괜찮은 거 같아

098

That's fine (with me)

(난) 괜찮아

099

That will be fine

괜찮아질 거야

100

That's okay (with me)

괜찮아, 난 상관없어

101

Are you all right?

괜찮아?

All right?은 「알겠니?」라고 상대방에게 물어보는 말.

102 Are you okay?

괜찮아?

103 Is it all right?

괜찮겠어? 괜찮아?

104 I'm cool with[about] that

난 괜찮아, 상관없어

105 Are you cool with this?

이거 괜찮아?

106 I can live with that

괜찮아, 참을 만해

I'm cool with that과 같은 맥락의 표현으로 의미는 It's okay with me 혹은 I will agree with that이다.

107 It works for me

난 괜찮아, 찬성이야

108 I have no problem with that

난 괜찮아요

109 It suits me (fine)

난 좋아, 내 생각엔 괜찮은 것 같아

110 I'm easy (to please)

네 결정에 따를게, 난 어느 쪽도 상관없어

111 I'm happy either way

난 아무거나 좋아

112 Either will do

아무거나 괜찮아

8 상대방의 말에 적극적으로 찬성하는 표현들

113 Be my guest

그럼요

114 Whatever you ask

뭐든 말만 해

115 Whatever you say

말만해, 전적으로 동감이야

116 Whatever you want to do

네가 하고 싶은 거 뭐든 좋아

117 Whatever it takes

무슨 수를 써서라도

118 Whatever turns you on

뭐든 좋을 대로

119 I am all yours

얼마든지, 뭐든지 다

120 Suit yourself

마음대로 해

121 You name it

말만 해

122 You are on

그래 좋았어

특히 내기를 받아들일 경우에 쓰는 표현.

123 So be it

(그렇게 결정됐다면) 그렇게 해

124 Anything you say

말만 하셔

125 Anytime

언제든지

부정

COMMON
SENTENCES
IN SITUATION
ENGLISH

9 생각 좀 해본다고 하면서 시간을 벌기

126 I'll think about it
그거에 대해 생각해볼게

127 I'll think it over
검토해볼게

128 Let me think about it
생각 좀 해볼게

129 Let me have time to think it over
생각할 시간 좀 줘

130 We're having second thoughts about it
다시 생각해봐야겠어

131 Let me sleep on it
곰곰이 생각해봐야겠어

132 I'll see what I can do
내가 어떻게 할 수 있는지 좀 보고

133 I never looked at it that way before

전에 그렇게 생각해 본 적이 없는데

10 상대방의 말에 가볍게 부정하기

134 I don't think so

그런 것 같지 않은데

135 I don't believe so

그런 것 같지 않은데

136 I guess not

아닌 것 같아

137 I suppose not

아닐 걸

138 I expect not

아닌 것 같아

139 I'm afraid not

아닌 것 같아

140 I'm afraid (that) 주어+동사

…가 아닌 것 같아

I'm afraid it's too late for that now 지금 그거 내세우기에는 너무 늦었다고 봐

141 I don't see that

난 그렇게 생각 안하는데, 그런 것 같지 않아

142 I don't see it (that way)

난 그렇게 생각하지 않아

143 I don't see that happening

그렇게는 안될 걸

144 That can't happen

말도 안돼, 그렇지 않아

145 I can't say 주어+동사

…라곤 말 못하지

I can't say he is innocent 걔가 무죄라고는 말 못하지

146 It's not what you think

그건 네 생각과 달라, 속단하지 마라

147 That's what you think

그건 네 생각이고

148 This is a totally different situation
전혀 다른 상황야

149 That's another[a different] story
그건 또 다른 얘기야, 그건 또 별개의 문제야

150 I have a different opinion
내 생각은 달라

151 Speak for yourself
그건 그쪽 얘기죠, 당신이나 그렇지

152 Not me
난 아냐

153 I wouldn't do that
나라면 그렇게 안하겠어

154 I didn't do it
내가 안 했어

155 I didn't cause this
내가 이런 건 아냐

156 Me neither

나도 안그래

157 Neither did I

나도 안그랬어

158 Neither do I

나도 안그래

159 Neither am I

나도 안그래

160 Neither will I

나도 안 그럴 거야

161 Neither can I

나도 못해

05 거절·반대

11 상대방의 부탁/제안을 가볍게 거절하기

162 I wish I could, but I can't

그러고 싶지만 안되겠어

163 I'd like to, but I'm on call today

그러고 싶은데, 난 오늘 대기해야 돼

I'd like[love] to, but~ 그러고 싶지만…

164 I'd have to say no

안되겠는데

165 I don't feel like it

사양할래, 그러고 싶지 않아

166 I'm sorry, but I don't have any money with me right now

미안하지만 지금 수중에 돈이 하나도 없어

I'm sorry, but~ 미안하지만…

167 No, thank you

고맙지만 사양하겠어요

168 No, thanks

고맙지만 됐어요

169 Nothing for me, thanks

고맙지만 난 됐어요

170 I'd rather not

그러고 싶지 않아

171 I'd rather you didn't

안그랬으면 좋겠는데

172 Not right now, thanks

지금은 됐어요

173 Not now

지금은 아냐

174 Not here

여기서는 말고

175 Not always

항상 그런 건 아니야

¹⁷⁶ **Not exactly**

꼭 그런 건 아니야

¹⁷⁷ **Not really**

실제로는 아니야

¹⁷⁸ **Not yet**

아직은 아냐

¹⁷⁹ **Not anymore**

이젠 됐어, 지금은 아니야

¹⁸⁰ **I don't think it was very good**

안 좋았다고 생각해

¹⁸¹ **That (all) depends**

상황에 따라 다르지, 경우에 따라 달라

Chapter 17

12 상대방의 부탁/제안에 직설적으로 거절하기

¹⁸² **I think you're wrong**

네가 틀렸다고 생각해

183 You're dead wrong

넌 완전히 틀렸어

184 You got the wrong idea

틀린 생각이야

185 You're on the wrong track

네가 잘못 생각했어

186 You're way off the mark

네가 아주 어긋났어

187 That's not right

그렇지 않아

188 It doesn't work

제대로 안돼, 그렇게는 안돼

189 It doesn't work that way

그렇게는 안 통해

190 It won't work

효과가 없을거야

191

That's not true

그렇지 않아, 사실이 아니야

192

I won't

싫어, 그렇게 안할래

193

Let's not

그렇게 하지 말자

194

It's not a good idea

별로 좋은 생각이 아니야

195

I can't do anything about it

어쩔 수가 없어

196

I can't make that happen

그렇게는 안되지

197

I don't buy it

못 믿어

198

We aren't buying your story

네 얘기 믿을 수 없어

199 I can't accept that

인정 못해

200 That's not how it works

그렇게는 안돼

201 That's not how we do things here

여기선 그렇게 하는 게 아냐

202 I don't[can't] agree with that[you]

그거에[네게] 동의할 수 없어

13 상대방의 부탁, 제안 등에 강하게 거절하기

203 No way!

절대 안돼!, 말도 안돼!

204 Not on your life!

결사반대야, 절대 안돼!

205 No, no, a thousand times no!

무슨 일이 있어도 안돼, 절대로 싫어

206 Not by a long shot

어떠한 일이 있어도 아냐, 어림도 없지

207 Not a thing

전혀

208 No, not a bit

아니, 조금도 안돼

209 Not that way!

그런식으론 안돼!

210 Not a chance!

안돼!

211 (There is) No chance!

안돼!

212 I said no

안 된다고 했잖아, 아니라고 했잖아

213 I'm dead set against it

난 결사 반대야

214 It's out of the question

그건 불가능해, 절대 안돼

215 No means no

아니라면 아닌 거지

216 Over my dead body

내 눈에 흙이 들어가기 전엔 안돼

217 That's impossible

그건 불가능해

218 It's never going to happen

그건 절대 안돼

happen 대신에 work를 써도 된다.

219 It's not even a possibility

절대 그런 일 없을거야

06 알아

14 상대방의 말에 나도 알고 있다고 말하기

220 I know (that)

알아, 알고 있어

I know는 이미 알고 있다(I had that information already)라는 의미이고 I see는 상대방이 뭔가 설명하거나 보여주고나서 이해했다(I understand)라는 의미로 쓰인다.

221 I know what I'm saying

나도 알고 하는 말이야, 내가 알아서 얘기한다구

222 I know what I'm talking about

나도 다 알고 하는 얘기야

223 I know what I'm doing

나도 아니까 걱정하지마, 내가 다 알아서 해

224 Do you know what you're doing?

잘 알겠지?, 어떻게 하는지 알지?

225 I've been there

무슨 말인지 충분히 알겠어, 정말 그 심정 이해해, 가본 적 있어

226 We have all been there

우리도 다 그런 적 있잖아

227 Been there done that

(전에도 해본 것이어서) 뻔할 뻔자지

228 I can see it in your eyes

네 눈에 그렇게 쓰여 있어

229 It's written all over your face

네 얼굴에 다 쓰여있어

상황별 영어
대표문장

07 몰라

15 아무도 모른다고 강하게 반어적으로 말해보기

230
Who knows?

누가 알겠어?

231
Who knows what could happen?

무슨 일이 일어날 지 어떻게 알아?

Who knows what[where] ~? 무엇이[어디서] …한지 누가 알아?

232
Who can tell?

누가 알겠어?

233
Nobody knows

아무도 몰라

234
God (only) knows!

누구도 알 수 없지!

235
Heaven[Lord; Christ] knows!

아무도 몰라!

236
That's anybody's guess

아무도 몰라

Chapter 17

237 # There's no way to tell

알 길이 없어

16 ## 상대방의 물음에 잘 모르겠다고 말하기

238 # I have no idea

몰라

239 # I have no idea what you just said

네가 무슨 말 하는지 전혀 모르겠어

240 # I didn't know that

모르고 있었지 뭐야

241 # I don't know about that

글쎄

242 # I don't know for sure

확실히 모르겠는데

243 # I don't know for certain

확실히 몰라

242
I'm not sure
잘 모르겠어

245
I'm not sure about that
그건 잘 모르겠는데

246
I'm not sure I agree with you
네 말이 맞는지 모르겠어

I'm not sure 주어+동사 …를 잘 모르겠어

247
I can't say (for sure)
잘 몰라, 확실히는 몰라

248
You got me
난 모르겠는데, 내가 졌어

249
You got me there
모르겠어, 네 말이 맞아

250
Beats me
잘 모르겠는데, 내가 어떻게 알아

251
Search me
난 몰라

Chapter 17

252 Not that I know of

내가 알기로는 그렇지 않아

253 Not likely

그럴 것 같지 않은데

254 Don't ask me

나한테 묻지마

255 Your guess is as good as mine

모르긴 나도 매한가지야

256 I don't understand (it)

왜 그런지 모르겠어, 알 수가 없네

257 I don't see why

이유를 몰라

17 나도 몰라, 나도 어쩔 수 없다고 말해보기

258 How should I know?

내가 어떻게 알아?

259   How can I tell?

내가 어떻게 알아?

260   What can I do?

내가 (달리) 어쩌겠어?

261   What more[else] can I do?

달리 방도가 있어?

262   What can I tell you?

뭐라고 얘기하면 되지?, 어쩌라구?

263   What can I say?

난 할 말이 없네, 나더러 어쩌라는 거야?, 뭐랄까?

264   What do you want me to say?

무슨 말을 하라는 거야? 나보고 어쩌라고?

265   (I) Can't help it

나도 어쩔 수 없어

266   It can't[couldn't] be helped

어쩔 수 없[었]어

267 I'm sorry, but I couldn't help it

미안하지만 어쩔 수가 없었어

268 You tell me

그거야 네가 알지

269 I wouldn't know

내가 알 도리가 없지, 그걸 내가 어떻게 알아

270 I have no other choice but to do so

그렇게 하는 거 외에는 달리 방법이 없어

271 I had no choice (in that matter)

그 문제에서 달리 방법이 없어

272 It was my only choice

나의 유일한 선택이었어

273 I don't have a clue

전혀 모르겠어

274 There was nothing else I could've done

달리 방법이 없어